SERIOUS LEISURE AND INDIVIDUALITY

Serious Leisure and Individuality

ELIE COHEN-GEWERC AND

ROBERT A. STEBBINS

McGill-Queen's University Press

Montreal & Kingston • London • Ithaca

© McGill-Queen's University Press 2013

ISBN 978-0-7735-4128-3 (cloth)
ISBN 978-0-7735-8848-6 (ePDF)
ISBN 978-0-7735-8849-3 (ePUB)

Legal deposit second quarter 2013
Bibliothèque nationale du Québec

Printed in Canada on acid-free paper that is 100% ancient forest free
(100% post-consumer recycled), processed chlorine free

McGill-Queen's University Press acknowledges the support of
the Canada Council for the Arts for our publishing program.
We also acknowledge the financial support of the Government
of Canada through the Canada Book Fund for our publishing
activities.

Library and Archives Canada Cataloguing in Publication

Cohen-Gewerc, Elie
    Serious leisure and individuality / Elie Cohen-Gewerc and Robert
A. Stebbins.

Includes bibliographical references and index.
Also issued in electronic format.
ISBN 978-0-7735-4128-3 (cloth). – ISBN 978-0-7735-8848-6 (ePDF). –
ISBN 978-0-7735-8849-3 (ePUB).

    1. Individuality – Social aspects. I. Stebbins, Robert A., 1938–
II. Title.

BF697.5.S65C63 2013   302.5'4   C2013-900033-X

Typeset by Jay Tee Graphics Ltd. in 10/13 Sabon

À Edith et Karin

Contents

Preface   ix

Introduction   3

1   Freedom and Being Free   11

2   Leisure Space: Cradle of the Individuated Person   29

3   Inclination to Play   64

4   Leisure and Consumption   81

5   Art in the Leisure Era   101

6   Community, Citizenship, and Globalization   119

Conclusion   145

Notes   157

Bibliography   163

Index   175

Preface

This book looks into those conditions in the modern world that make for individuality, or individual distinctiveness, and the place of these conditions in personal and social life. We approach individuality first by examining its relationship with freedom and being free. Next, we define and elaborate the concept of leisure space, treating it as the cradle of individuality. After this we consider, in three separate chapters, the role of play, consumption, and art in inhibiting or generating individuality. Since individuality has an array of consequences extending beyond the individual, we also examine its place in community, citizenship, and globalization.

In all this, we do not look on individuality as an unalloyed good. We also consider its negative side and its negative consequences, both for the individual and for her society. In this same vein, we examine the complex relationship between individuality and alienation.

There are many books on the modern individual, which centre, however, almost entirely on the person vis-à-vis her local community and broader society. The principal interest of these books lies in distinguishing the individual from her immediate community and broader society, and in many instances, showing how the contemporary individual has arisen as an entity distinct from her community and society where she was once a more obscure element. The Beck/Beck-Gernsheim thesis on individualization (*Individualization*, published in 2002), which argues that modern actors are responsible for their own lives and the consequences of their performances, exemplifies this line of thinking. In other words, such analyses have separated the parts from the whole, arguing that the parts have, in modern times, become at least as important and as visible as the whole. The point of reference in this line of analysis is the individual seen against the backdrop of society.

We take this approach a step further. In effect we ask the following question: Now that we have learned that modern individuals stand out from society and cannot today be seen as merely one of many cogs in a machine, what makes them stand out from each other? Thus, our point of comparison is not society, but rather the other individuals whom, in their everyday lives, people meet or know of. This said, we do include a chapter on individuality in community, citizenship, and globalization.

In short, our study of individuality differs from those of individualism and individualization, primarily because the main points of comparison diverge considerably. True, scholars studying individualism and individualization occasionally touch selectively on aspects of individuality, even while their comparative reference is society. What is missing in the literature and what we intend to provide in this book is a broad, comprehensive examination of individuality, particularly as it roots substantially in leisure and certain areas of work where it is most like leisure. That is, serious leisure and devotee work can, compared with other kinds of work and leisure, offer the most profound bases for modern individuality, as well as a profound personal emancipation from the commonplace temptations of individualism that sometimes lead to alienation – and the need to escape from alienation.

THE PHILOSOPHICAL AND SOCIOLOGICAL PERSPECTIVES

The broad treatment of individuality promised in this book cannot be effected through either philosophy or sociology alone, the disciplines in which the two authors were trained. The subject demands examination through the lens of both, which is the approach we have taken. Rather than trying to force the relevant philosophical and sociological concepts, principles, and observations into a disciplinary Procrustean bed, we have purposely retained their distinctive intellectual provenance, including presenting them in the literary style of the discipline in question: so it is that chapters 1, 3, and 5 are philosophical and were written by Cohen-Gewerc, whereas chapters 2, 4, and 6 are sociological and were written by Stebbins. Both authors reviewed and occasionally added to the other's chapters. And both authors had a hand in writing the introduction and conclusion. Such a facture risks being piecemeal, but nonetheless, we believe that we have written a coherent work – that the two lenses have produced a coherent image, albeit a complex one. This image clearly portrays the nature of individualization in the twenty-first century.

ACKNOWLEDGMENTS

We wish to thank Jacqueline Mason for effectively shepherding our manuscript through the review process in its many phases. James Thomas handled with consummate literary expertise and admirable patience the copyediting of this book, a work that spans the disciplines of philosophy, sociology, and leisure studies and that has intellectual foundations in English and French sources. In writing it, the authors frequently worked back and forth in the two languages. We deeply appreciate the efforts of these two fine representatives of McGill-Queen's University Press.

SERIOUS LEISURE AND INDIVIDUALITY

Introduction

In the glorification of "work" and the never-ceasing talk about the "blessing of labour," I see the same secret *arrière-pensée* as I do in the praise bestowed on impersonal acts of a general interest, viz. a fear of everything individual. ... And now, horror of horrors! it is the "workman" himself who has become dangerous; the whole world is swarming with "dangerous individuals," and behind them follows the danger of dangers – the individuum!

Nietzsche, *The Dawn of Day*, §173[1]

THE TRIUMPH OF THE INDIVIDUAL: A PYRRHIC VICTORY?

For centuries, we were told – from the moment we first opened our eyes and throughout our initiation and supervision by society – who and what we had to be. The challenge was to avoid any kind of personal aspirations one could have thought of by one's self. People were considered to be a sort of raw material, a collection of spare parts for the maintenance and durability of the community, and mostly they agreed. In other words, people belonged to society, and any embryo of self-awareness had to be seen as illegitimate.

Nowadays, even among traditional communities, it is quite rare, however, to ignore the fact that every individual has, and must have, personal views – and a will of his own. This evolution towards individuality began in the Western world in the early Renaissance, where life emerged from being considered a simple corridor leading to the next world. More and more, we saw life as a great "lounge" where we could enjoy the moment and realize our desires and aspirations for the sake of our existence here and now – and no longer only for the sake of the Last Judgment. In this process, artist and student communities were the early pioneers of the emerging sense of individuality. Artists began to autograph their creations, at this time, so as to show their uniqueness, looking for personal recognition. More and more individuals went on their own path, slightly separated from the main and compulsory road. Fighting for their different views, their different perceptions, they would introduce into ever more minds the seeds of what eventually invaded everybody's awareness and received the acknowledgment of institutions – the human right to be one's self, an individual. Wars, struggles, and revolutions would lead to a great variety of declarations claiming the rights of distinct groups and, above all, of individuals.

This has been a long process that has its own track record, in parallel with, or in response to, many other developments in society. As in all periods, for example, despite the existence today of globalizing cultural networks, we can observe how a great diversity of cultures and mentalities have coexisted and, many times, in the same country – someone can live in France or England, the original homes of individual freedom, and be confronted by traditions far less progressive.

We can imagine a sort of scale, from the total negation of the individual to express his or her individuality to the total legitimacy of being one's self. At the freer end of the scale, we observe how parents and educators have tried to attend to every tendency and talent of a child, offering him the opportunity to express himself and to experience a range of various types of training. At the other, more restrictive end, we observe very young children enclosed in a narrow existence of controlled and established socialization from dawn to dusk, disconnected from any kind of knowledge that does not fit the beliefs and the aims of the community.

Yet knowledge of the variety of existing alternatives filters through. This is something closely analogous to the process that has changed totally the distribution of goods in the world today. Who doesn't remember the small grocery where a few articles were always kept behind the counter, under the strict control of the clerk? What remains of this authoritarian control in those hypermarkets with their innumerable articles, all freely available to everyone? We can see how the whole world seems to be a huge supermarket of opportunities offered, in theory, to the free will of any individual. More and more students, for instance, now have the opportunity to go shopping for a university education around the globe.

Individuals can throughout much of the world look freely for anything and go easily everywhere, for those open, global networks run to every taste. A consequence of this process is that individuals now enjoy access to a multitude of organizations, suppliers, dealers, publishers that can bypass what remains of the weakened authority of parents, teachers, and community leaders.

As we understand this, however, it does not mean that people now live in an era of personal freedom and autonomy. In most cases individuals have never emancipated themselves from the compulsory influence of community and social frames. They have simply lost it. Note how flocks of people try to join any trend, any fashion, looking for some equivalent of social belonging, something that can provide an acceptable identity, even if only fragile and temporary. You can belong to a group of people who share the same hobby, join an ad hoc committee to prevent the destruction of an old building (for the sake of its heritage), or even just talk about the latest restaurant or TV program in vogue. All this can provide the rewarding feeling of belonging, without the accompaniment of duty.

Although the world has changed profoundly, most people still need this kind of social pattern. The great difference is the huge flexibility of what we will call "modular conformism," whose essence consists in always being free for the next proposal, the next social movement. Like stones in a pathway, individuals need to feel strong as part of a framed world, even if they have to accept some amount of social pressure inside the relevant group. They tend, therefore, to join any interest or cause capable of attracting a lot of adherents. Being "trendy" also inspires an image of freedom and relevancy, and modular conformity seems to be an easy alternative to traditional social frameworks, free of any aspect of a life commitment that has lost its raison d'être.

Beyond the conquest of legitimacy, we have to see how people in their actual circumstances deal with the opportunity of being different and unique. Today, it is not enough to refer to abstract values. We must consider the vital presence in people's minds of local norms and historical conditions (Honneth 1995). A whole century ago, Georg Simmel (1989) said that the idea of a personality absolutely free and unique was not the last word. He believed that the "immense work of Humanity" would be to create new and more multitudinous forms of human existence, and that through these diverse forms, each one's personality would assert itself and the value of its existence (304). To be sure, the twentieth century was a creative one. But the task is far from over! What are the conditions and what factors would facilitate this "immense work of humanity"?

That is the issue!

Would this vast work of humanity include the contemporary atomization of society, leaving alienated individuals who have become easy targets to be enrolled, first by huge ideological movements, and later by any kind of fleeting trend? Is there any conceivable way out of the dilemma of being trapped by a strictly defined identity or casually or vaguely addicted to a life of individualistic consumerism?

From innumerable vantage points all over the world, the Western world particularly, we can perceive how hard, how colossal the challenge is of being free. Apprehensive, faced with confused concepts, with uncertainty regarding the future, we are still "condemned to be free" (Sartre 1943), looking for any kind of consistency and above all, some identity – at least for immediate use – or at least some substitute for it. People have wanted, and still want, to be recognized as having the prerogative to be different and to decide for themselves without constraints, but they also want some safety nets, just in case. In their struggle – that is, their "struggle for recognition" (Honneth 1995) – they demand for themselves the "capacity to express needs and desires without fear of being abandoned as a result" (xiii). The classic example would be the young adult refusing any advice and even less, any intervention ("Don't tell me what to do!") but ready to return to the childhood condition of being allowed to call at two o'clock in the morning: "Dad I have a problem here, you must come!"

There is a great misunderstanding about the enjoyment of liberty: struggles for recognition and legitimacy are enshrined in all the charters of human rights – which, however, tend to minimize the other part of the equation bearing on duties and commitments. In line with Charles Taylor (*Sources of the Self* [1989]), who doesn't wonder what basis we could have to realize our aspirations to benevolence and universal justice, when we know how the best of such aspirations have led to many terrible, cruel regimes and crimes? We may say the same thing, however, about the many "terrible, cruel" deeds of individuals. In this book, we will try to show that a path to one's individuality does not go only through the exclusive acquisition of rights and privileges, but includes the consciousness of one's personal commitment to what we would term, "humankind *oblige*."[2] This is the essence of a freedom that no longer seems a condemnation: "Life lived in freedom is personal responsibility or it is a pathetic farce" (Buber 1955, p. 92).

We also understand that the essence of social and human issues lies in how individuals and communities perceive the concepts of identity and freedom. For all those who don't see themselves as defined by any clear-cut ideology, the central issue remains one of self-identity. You dream of being somebody. You discover you are various somebodies or even nobody. What a discovery! But is this a finishing or starting point? A deadlock or an invitation to further discovery?

Surprisingly, many people would appear to deny that well-being demands any effort, essentially any effort to choose – to choose what we want to be, instead of being chosen, drawn out by trends and changing circumstances. It is not enough to dream or even to aspire to be somebody. We need to make a concrete effort, first to assume what we really are, then to break off with the one we would "cease to be" (González Pecotche 1934, 13). Only from that platform of the self can we realize our inner identity, which we discover through our genuine, elaborate encounters with other people and innumerable other aspects of life – around us and within ourselves.

Then every personal encounter should be part of one's further search for one's self, as one attends to the resonating affects of each new encounter – as a chemist, to discover the properties of a new substance, generates various "meetings" with other substances, making it interact with them to observe the results. To discern, to apprehend, to feel, to understand, to know the decisive prerogatives of our personal freedom in every experience is the only way leading to our essential individuality. We are referring to a dynamic and moving identity emerging from a perpetually "self-making tailor," and far from all the fashionable, casual, ready-to-wear identities.

However, most of us will question: How can we become involved in such a process while we are entirely seized with our struggle for survival? It is like the "watch" dilemma of Friedrich Schiller in the third of his *Letters upon the Aesthetic Education of Man*: "When the mechanic has to mend a watch, he lets the wheels run out, but the living watchworks of the state have to be repaired while they act, and a wheel has to be exchanged for another during its revolutions" ([1794] 1909–14). Is it possible to "change the wheel during its revolution," and build a new self? In other words, how can I continue to assume my non-essential identity (a result of fortuity and happenstance) while creating a new one? Couldn't leisure space, thanks to its specific characteristics, offer new opportunities of being who we genuinely desire to be?

Leisure time means open-ended ways of relating and new conceptions of the individual, enlarged legitimacy, and recognition of more diverse social visions of life. It means the multiplication of the sources of accessible knowledge and social exchanges totally free from any dependence for vital and social survival. Are we ready for that? Have we the skills to deal with all these variables? Are we able to manage this avalanche of stimuli? Are we prepared to use this special breathing space and create the necessary distance for this serene practice of being free?

The new era of leisure and all its new concepts are already quite with us, but we are still anchored in the state of mind of the "old world." We will need to move from a standard, quite passive condition of adaptation towards a creative one. The era of leisure can be a sort of vertigo of casual forms of distraction in which one can become lost, but it can also be a privileged space of self-re-education. Many of the sophisticated tools of aggressive marketing, which serve the interests of unfettered capitalism throughout the world today, could also help creating new solidarities, new axes of humanity where everyone could be an individual with, and for, their human partners.

But, first of all, we have to elucidate what is really entailed in being one's self. Can we establish a stable identity running with or against trends and fashions? Are we dealing with "personality" (a socially alloted image of one's self) or "individuality" (one's genuine self) (González Pecotche 1998)? Can we discern and bring together the particular and universal in our identity? We will also try to see to what extent leisure space can nurture and be the cradle of the individual. How can the individual we aspire to be, cohabit with our consumer culture? What happens to the concept of community when individuality emerges? And what about being only one of more than 7 billion people (as of 2011) in the world today?

If we are right to speak of a new era of leisure, we must review all of our concepts, such as "work" and its new place in personal life; "time," which is no longer only money; "body" and the meaning of age; "countries and states," "homelands," and the supermarket of landscapes and populations; "aesthetics" and its contributions to individuality, uniqueness, and human solidarity; and "life" as a wide scene of perpetual searching and hoping, including personal and essential happiness.

All the ingredients seem to be there: infinite sources of knowledge, innumerable networks of human contacts, and multiple possibilities to express oneself and be the self-author of one's unique individuality. Of course, shallow and ready-to-use individualism is also present and has all the means to alienate potential individuality, which needs to be created and improved. The leisure state of mind can promote – beyond the instinctive reaction of the escapism supported and encouraged by the leisure industries – a moving re-encounter with our essential selves, towards a fruitful dialogue with life.

Our purpose is to show how the leisure era, and all the new approaches to life it entails, can offer the opportunity to empower one's unique individuality and overcome the trap of individualism's abyss. We will show how we can be the worthy heirs of those who have struggled throughout the centuries for the recognition of their individuality.

I

Freedom and Being Free

Being free as a bird, as in the Beatles song, is an idea that has inspired people throughout the ages.

We see the bird take off elegantly, take off far from the confined topography of human life. We look at it gliding peacefully, so far away from earthly worries.

How can we, rooted in life's circumstances, prevent our soul from going after the light movements of the bird?

Long live freedom! Let's reach out for happiness!

What longing! What confusion!

We work so hard, sacrifice a lot, and pay a high price trying to rebel against the decisions of parents, teachers, governors, and their employees who prevent us from attaining what we consider our individualistic happiness.

We haven't discovered yet that our real subjugation is to our beliefs, our prejudices, and the decisive statements that determine life.

Like the bird that gives itself up to the limited space that ensures refuge and food, the individual sees the views commonly held by those around him as the bars of a mental cage, providing a protected but sterile existence.

For the important issue is not the bird but the precious inner being. It is our responsibility to offer this inner being the possibility of rising up above the common life where we splash about, existence captured in mortgaged time.

There, on high, when we attain freedom, we will discover, in our inner and intimate being's landscapes, the virgin spaces of a potential self.

To fly far away to our selves: that can be also the great lesson of the bird which flies through the landscape of our life, especially when time becomes free.

The word "leisure," contemplated by itself, invites one to enter into a delightful mood of freedom.[1]

Yet, which concept of freedom springs out in our minds? Are we sure that freedom is always synonymous with pleasure? Where does this freedom disappear to when leisure is over? On the other hand, what happens when circumstances force us to be outside of our familiar and well-known space, disconnected from roles and obligations, from the tacit but essential legitimacy of our existence? Do we conceive our freedom to be the basic axis of our human condition? Sometimes it seems that this whole issue remains a virtual one, until we genuinely and personally confront the fact that we are free (Sartre 1943). "Freedom" is a word that is much overused, misused, manipulated, and terribly challenging to define. Freedom accompanies life as an unarticulated background, while we embroider the cloth of time with roles, tasks, obligations – as if on a kind of autopilot. Freedom becomes acutely present at times when our schedule tends to be empty, when free time makes it clear to us how difficult it is to be free, to face up to what appears to be a void.

FREEDOM AND LEISURE

Freedom becomes a serious and major challenge, once we step across the threshold of significant leisure space. We are here beyond the narrow definition of leisure, dividing one's time into time making a living and the time remaining. This tendency of the narrow conceptualization of time inherited from Judeo-Christian beliefs appears occasionally as a dichotomy, such as the religious division of life into sacred and secular.[2] Entering this new realm of leisure, we are beyond such a simple approach to time. We no longer exist in these small breaks, these narrow bridges between roles; instead, we enter, as it were, a great lounge, emptied of functions and duties. While Sartre (1955) said that the looks others direct towards us are what weave the web of hell,[3] a far worse situation is to be distanced from these same looks, ejected from those comfortable refuges in others' approving eyes. We are then confronted, alone,[4] with our entire human condition, essentially with our freedom.

The passage from a tight schedule full of commitments, where an individual knows what he has to do and knows what he is expected to be, to white empty pages in a superfluous diary can be a hard encounter with one's freedom. To all this, we must add that behind the previously intense activity, when the agenda was totally overbooked, we were not really assured of clear-cut concepts, nor of any well-defined identity. We discover then that landing in the wide open space of leisure does not mean that we are actually able to be free. Mostly we experience a kind of exile, far from our familiar territory, our well-known "kingdom." In fact, nothing has changed, the only change that has occurred is in our point of view.

This kind of exile begins when we have to look at life directly, without the intermediate repertoire of apparently obvious roles, obligations, and tasks. How does the seemingly obvious come to appear not so obvious after all? How does it happen that I suddenly feel in exile in the middle of what I had considered, till that instant, my familiar realm? How do some see what others fail to recognize? You must remember that the optical organ does not make us see; on the contrary, we are the ones who make our eyes capable of seeing, according to our degree of awareness. In what appears to be our seemingly obvious, self-evident, but ultimately false, "kingdom," we tend to move on the surface of life, led by habits and routines full of events, agitations, and distractions – which can fill the whole chronological time of an entire life. Against this background, leisure can suddenly be a kind of catalyst for something more, a privileged crossroads at which I can surmise the veiled parts of life, the hidden essence of potential life, and the small relevance of what used to be "important" things.

It can also be a stressful experience when free time becomes emptiness, demanding to be filled up to substitute for one's former schedule. There are so many choices, so many suggestions, so many temptations waiting for us to decide on – entirely our responsibility. How can the individual navigate through life, when overwhelmed by an overdose of invasive choices with, as background, the chaos of the former, outwardly obvious awareness? One can be in the type of high-risk zone that Ehrenberg calls freedom's disease, when freedom is "symbolically open to all possibilities" (2000, 35), and individual abilities are often so limited. Yet, sometimes one can surprise oneself, wondering: perhaps my essential way of life is not to be found in this flood of commodities, trends, and leisure fashions and I have to create it for and by myself? Some pale reminiscence of passing desires I experienced in the course of my life?

From time to time, a bud of freedom emerges in a sudden pulse of leisure within a structured schedule, out of the established and dense agenda. Franz Kafka, in a very short story, describes the case of someone who decides to act in opposition to an established routine. He is at the end of his daily ritual and expecting to go to bed when he suddenly starts up, changes his jacket and goes out. Then he experiences his legs enjoying this "unexpected liberty" and above all his greater strength to decide and behave against familiar expectations. These vanished from his awareness as he sensed himself "a firm, boldly drawn black figure, slapping himself on the thigh, grow to his true stature."[5]

Kafka's character discovers his own freedom – listening to his own body, which whispered about the unexpected liberty he had procured, discovering he was more than he expected he could be; he suddenly discovered himself and was able to "grow to his true stature." It is interesting to imagine what would happen to this man. Would he come back to his regular, scheduled life and regard this event as unique, accidental, or would this small walk outside the norm become a departure to a new era, a new vision. In other words, was this small happening part of casual leisure or a vital invitation to enter into the vast realm of serious leisure?

We all have these kinds of experiences, which are like signals reminding us that life is greater than the small parts of it expressed in our various roles: we all hope that the surgeon who sees only a small segment of the body, and focuses his attention on one organ, likewise does not forget that surrounding a specific organ lies a whole human being and his entire world.

How does one respond to these appeals to the whole coming up from one's hidden self?

That is the issue!

What happens after these encounters with freedom? What occurs when this becomes a permanent breakthrough, when the sense of freedom refuses to die away?

DISCOVERING FREEDOM

The discovery of freedom is neither a final nor a definitive result. On the contrary, it points out the real beginnings of our search for our selves and the discovery of all the implications of this dramatic event. This dramatic event has nothing to do with the non-essential state of mind in which it seems that I "can do something or nothing at all, just feeling free" (Iso-Ahola 2009, 139).

"Just feeling free" indicates most often that we have entered a special no man's land, with no constraints, no controls, no judgments. Here we feel that we have acquired a sort of immunity, being beyond sanctions of any kind. Thus, according to Suetonius, the Roman emperor Caligula "felt free" to promote somebody and then dismiss him the day after; sometimes he even condemned him to death. He could nominate anybody to be senator, even his beloved horse. In the play by Albert Camus, Caligula argues that in doing so he sought to be like the gods, who can do whatever they desire without any obligation to render an account! But at the end of the play, at the last instant before being assassinated, Caligula concludes, "I have chosen a wrong path, a path that leads to nothing. My freedom isn't the right one" (Camus 1965, 97).

Very often, people discover a freedom that "isn't the right one." Victims of their narrow minds, they rush through all the fences, thinking that freedom consists of a world without prohibitions. Their discovery of themselves as free is limited to external circumstances, and freedom becomes synonymous with permissiveness. Permissiveness means that people do not really acquire freedom but only lose their social framework. Their "being free" looks to them like the first joy of children whose parents are not at home.

They have a lot of fun, eat what they wish, organize a great battle with all the pillows, laugh a lot, enjoy fully the lack of parental supervision. But gradually their absence turns this euphoric sensation into anxiety. The children are no longer in a mood of "feeling free"; they experience the uneasy sensation of being abandoned! In this same perspective we can say that "the more the individual is freed and becomes the manager of himself, the more he seems to be vulnerable, fragile, internally disarmed" (Lipovetsky and Serroy 2008, 59).[6]

As Nietzsche too pointed out, through Zarathustra: "Free *from* what? What doth that matter to Zarathustra! Clearly, however, shall thine eye show unto me: free *for* what?" (1896, para. XVII). Freedom *from* is the path designed for individualism that triumphs on the ruins of traditional social ties, an individualism that reveals a weakened self, offered to non-essential and changing stimuli (Touraine 2005), casual and shallow leisure based on passive entertainment. This individualism has passed to a global scale, and tends to disorganize "consciences, ways of life, existences" (Lipovetsky and Serroy 2008, 19). Simply "feeling free" is far removed from a feeling of significant freedom. The encounter with significant freedom is a dramatic event in which the individual senses that expectations and supervision from outside have lost their impact, leaving it up to this individual to become a distinctive human being.

At this moment, I know that I know, and am self-consciously aware of the fact, that I'm free *for*. I am aware that my existence has to be considered as a whole and that "freedom obliges."

With the tangible discovery of freedom, I recover the ability to see: the capacity to discern more and more things, aspects, and nuances that had remained out of our field of vision, its having been totally filled with the contents of the small stage on which we were confined. The horizon becomes wider and wider and I can perceive how, on the one hand, central items of my daily life lose their primacy; on the other hand, my inner dialogue, the dialogue I have with myself, grows up and becomes the most relevant criterion for my evaluations, my choices, my deeds. I sense, intuitively, that my freedom is intrinsically linked with my uniqueness.

FREEDOM AS THE OPPORTUNITY OF BECOMING ONESELF

Within this new world of freedom, I become more permeable to new aspects and more attentive to my sensibility. I am able to transcend my automatic behaviour of yesterday.

Initially entering into a new realm of direct and personal perception, I am in the position of a newcomer, becoming a sort of stranger to my old network of beliefs and patterns. Standing outside of their closed influence, I am capable of distinguishing a lot of nuances I did not see when everything seemed so evident. Eugene Ionesco (1952) in his famous play, *The Bald Prima Dona*, presents two couples. Each of these couples exchange the surprising statements: "you are my wife"; "you are my husband." These obvious, trivial declarations sound as new as they do bizarre. By these "banal" phrases, these characters transform their unthinking, conventional commitment. A new commitment emerges from their freedom and in it is implied each one's personal and total responsibility.

Watching these dialogues as spectators we remember the stories where the hero, after some trauma, wakes up and asks, "Where am I?" Conscious of my freedom, I have to answer the basic question: "Who am I?" This is a crucial moment in which all the old parameters that could have helped to give one a satisfying identity have no longer any relevance, or at least very little.

To be free is to be the one whom I aspire to be, beyond all the external, circumstantial definitions, beyond all the roles I am or was ever committed to. Something occurs that I can perceive, still indistinctly, a kind of hope for self-expression and a vague expectation of being able to actualize myself. Occasionally we get some idea of what freedom can be when we meet people who seem to have had the good fortune to realize earnestly their deep desires during their free time, and we become aware of how leisure can be a serious issue. To feel free means that all paths are open, that all domains are potentially possible spaces for the revelation of my self. I am free from all patterns, ready to step in accordance with the light of my own understanding. This new wakefulness to a world beyond the self-evident, though it springs up as essential and personal, promotes a sort of promise beyond selfishness.

To discover, to apprehend, to understand, to sense, to be aware of the concept of freedom as it emerges in me, will be the premise of the fulfillment of my individuality, being then a concrete testimony of humanity, a necessary encouragement for the germination of the seeds of freedom hidden within me, within every man and woman. These are the seeds occasionally watered in times spent outside of the autopilot and made to germinate when someone transcends the ordinary sense of its leisure free time, turning it from the casual kind to the type of serious leisure we will analyze further.

The history of humankind is made up of the individual stories of these experiences, sources of inspiration for all those who dare to be themselves and assume their uniqueness, the genuine expression of their freedom. Experimenting with freedom leads us to become conscious of our humanity. "There are two forms," Buber observed, "indispensable for the building of true human life, to which the originative instinct, left to itself, does not lead and cannot lead: to sharing in an undertaking and to entering into mutuality" (1955, 87). Thus, we know that we cannot be free alone, we cannot realize our liberty in the shadow of an alienated humanity, where men and women are trapped far from their inner selves because "the demands of existence are there, making the power to choose simply an auxiliary of the need to live" (Bergson 1966, 20). Could we expect this pessimistic equation to change if we were in a space without necessity, by its nature: leisure time?

FREEDOM AND LEISURE – THE SECOND CHANCE

Leisure by its nature can be a great opportunity for the seeds of our freedom to germinate. Leisure is this time away, this "time-out," out of all roles, obligations, patterns.

Let us compare this with an extra amount of money, after all our payments. We can use it for any purpose, disconnected from any outside demand. The leader of any organization, company, or even any democratic state knows that a good 80–90 percent of the budget is allocated in advance, yet how many great things, reforms, creations could be done with this 10–20 percent of "free" money! This is a kind of new resource not yet designated, offered exclusively to our desire. We arrive at that crucial moment where we experience as our sole responsibility, how this free time sets us at the crossroads of our liberty.

Beyond any role, without a care, I'm aware that every decision I make – including doing nothing – will be no one else's responsibility but my own. Here I am: me and myself. What an encounter! What an opportunity! Or not?[7] Indeed this new state of mind, inspired by leisure can be our second chance, a second arrival, a new opening for our inner self.

We emerge into life in a world already laid down for us, where we understand very rapidly that our survival depends on our appearance in the eyes of the relevant others. The main issue will lie in being what I am expected to be, or more precisely, in behaving in harmony with the role I have to play in every scenario in my social life.[8] While step by step my personality builds itself as a mixture of inner tendencies and a whole repertoire of automatic aptitudes, a large part of me remains idle – a fallow land. In the human species' long and mostly unconscious journey towards survival – in its wide meaning – accustomed to being shaped by life like a common pebble by the flowing water of a river, humanity gets its outline as a result of all the elements acting outside of it. Nowadays we must add the potent factor of the media, which makes of our humanity "a monitor in which are screened the desires, needs, and imaginary worlds fabricated by the communications industries" (Touraine 2005).

In other words, we become what circumstances make us into, and we perceive ourselves through the image reflected in these mirrors all around, an image we try to upgrade constantly, at least outwardly. This maintenance demands every available energy, and we generally fall into a subtle and vicious cycle: as much as I invest in showing the personage that circumstances lead me to be, by the same token I remain distant from a large part of my authentic self, and sometimes totally alienated. Invaded by innumerable stimuli, I seldom have enough room to discern any reality beyond the requirements of my various roles.

Then something happens unexpectedly (or expectedly, but as repressed, long put out of mind – such as retirement) and I suddenly find myself pushed off the carousel of life. After an appreciable rest, I discover that there is nothing to accomplish, no role to fulfill, and nobody to satisfy. I sense myself in the heart of a vaguely defined present, in a kind of "loose" time that stretches out into an infinity of futurelessness (Jankélévitch 1963) in which I am abandoned to myself, *alone* with my freedom.

Before now, I could say that most of the time I did what I had to: paid attention only to what was relevant to my specific roles, decided what was adequate to my established trajectory – all in a sort of state of mind that "there is nothing to do" except what I'm induced to accomplish by what is expected of me. Things seemed to be pre-chosen in a quasi-automatic track, while freedom seemed to be a theoretic and vague concept, a virtual and ineffective background to actual life.

Yet, being alone with myself and with my freedom, I can discover that there are many aspects of actual life normally covered over by our disingenuous existence, many things moving inner and deeper chords unknown to me until the precise instant they appeared. The world now seems to be wider and I am able to hear, to smell, to sense all around, and overall in my essential self.[9] A magic space emerges in my consciousness: "leisure time" where life springs out of all the more accepted moulds, out of all the old thinking patterns. There we are finally able – at a low price and sometimes at no cost at all – to liberate ourselves from the place assigned to us.

This is a magic space where I can meet my whole self, with all those facets not formerly expressed, because they were not necessary to anyone, not necessary even to my former self. Being free means, now, that I can consider myself and my life as a whole, beyond the straight paths determined by the various tracks of survival; I am no longer just a pile of characters reflected in the eyes of others[10] and powered by tasks, missions, obligations, alien expectations, roles, and rules. I am no longer shaped like a river pebble; my freedom consists in being able to preside over my own changes, in becoming "a subject," that is, "not only one who says 'I' but a man who is conscious that he has the right to say 'I'" (Touraine 2005).

Leisure time is time without rules (Jankélévitch 1963), time that escapes from the moulds of conventional thought and moves away from the repertoire of familiar occupations. This is empty time, empty of all of what used to occupy one's customary mode of life. This is a moment when the void and the nothingness are revealed, in which the unique self will float up. This void is in fact a pregnant one – pregnant with infinite perspectives and voices whispering from backstage, behind the scenes of "normalized existence." Charles Baudelaire explained this well (1961, 62):

Sometimes one finds an old perfume bottle that still
    remembers,
From which bursts forth, full of life, a breath of scent.
A thousand old thoughts, like cold cocoons,
Reverberate heavily in the deep darkness
Then spread their wings and take flight.

There, in the lack of routine, one can meet the scent of a forgotten perfume that recalls one's uniqueness, the central point of one's essential existence – where concern arises. It is from here that one will awaken and a renewed vision will develop, a view that sees, looks, and observes from within, wonders about the unlimited richness of one's own existence, and of existence as a whole. Here, one will renew a kind of authentic affinity, whose peak will be the awareness of human solidarity, of total responsibility for nature, and the awareness of the spiritual dimension. Here we are no longer in the delimited contours of a readymade identity, whose narrowness cannot include all the new horizons we begin to distinguish.

The new feeling of freedom rests on the inner courage to face an unpredictable future, a future that draws those weary of the well-trodden pathways. This is the space that comes out with the discovery that *freedom obliges*, and invites us to be entirely what we aspire to be. Feeling free means then, that we can transcend the limits that seemingly determine our existence, seemingly forever, and that we can recover the greatest of all human treasures: the ability to create.

Being free is not a theoretical inference; it is not merely what I pretend, nor only what I desire, to be. To be free is what I intend to be. It implies, not merely a series of much needed vacations and breaks from routine, but essentially: creation. "If, in all domains," Bergson tells us, "life's triumph is creation, we should suppose that human life has its *raison d'être* in creation which can ... continue throughout life in every man: the creation of one's self by one's self, the expansion of personality by an effort that takes much out of little, something from nothing, and adds continuously to what there is of riches in the world" (1966, 24).

To be free is not a unique, one-off performance. Realizing freedom is a consistent purpose, a thought[11] carefully crafted; to understand this, it helps to keep an eye on our personal commitment to our part of humanity, as well as being conscious of what we name "freedom *oblige*." Keeping an eye on one's essential purpose includes a serene accompaniment, a continuous dialogue between me and myself. Becoming free is the infinite empowering process of our consciousness, assuming one's freedom is a lifelong endeavour.

It starts when I focus on my mind, when I succeed in creating some distance between myself and the world – an indispensable space to enable tranquil observation. It is like hugging someone we love, after a long absence – we "must," the instant after our first embrace, hold him or her off and contemplate, to be sure, to be aware, to be conscious of whether what we really feel is in harmony with what we think. We should likewise hold off facts and events, according to González Pecotche (1998), to pay a visit to our sanctuary within the mind, to our ensemble of thoughts. The quality of our life, the breadth of our vision, and the depth of our perception are always the results of the thoughts within us at any given moment, and of the degree of awareness we have of their potential impact. In parallel with our concern about what is going on around us, we should have a look at our inner world and observe the mental movements inside, this living and productive microcosm within.

The crucial place for our personal freedom is not in the external theatre of life. Rather, it happens behind the scenes, in our minds, where we try to be aware of all the thoughts accompanying and entering into our decisions. It includes some clear-cut (some not so clear-cut), alien suggestions, conflicts between thoughts and feelings, focused attention, and passive inertia. We all understand and agree that the quality of a performance on stage is the result of all the energy invested during the rehearsals. The rehearsals of our stage acts take place in our minds. To be free means that I am the director, that I know and govern all the "thoughts" involved in every future event, their relative impacts, and the relationships between them. My steadfast, tangible freedom begins in my mind and continues in the concrete alchemy whereby I choose those thoughts able to perform as I want them to.

My mind, then, is no longer a simply given concourse of thoughts, abandoned to indeterminate input from the circumstances surrounding me. It becomes my HQ, where I gather perceptions, discernments, understandings, intuitions, and insights into a personal and deliberate ensemble in harmony with my emerging and free individuality, for which I am responsible.

In the perspective of freedom, one is not only responsible for one's acts; one is also "responsible for [one's] thoughts" (González Pecotche 1998, 68), the thoughts dwelling in one's mind. Though, as we have said before, to be genuinely free – that is, to be conscious of our freedom – is never a final and definitive achievement. It's a fragile acquisition, needing constant attention and sustained care.

TO BE FREE MEANS BEING ALERT AND VIGILANTLY MINDFUL

Let us enter into a well-known icon of our contemporary world of consumption, a super- or hypermarket, where we can, in the nature of the case, fully enjoy our freedom. By contrast to the grocery of the past, where all the goods were kept behind a large front counter, totally controlled by the grocer, all the merchandise in today's hypermarket is accessible and we are "free" to step along the shelves, check every product and choose what will, or will not, "land" in our shopping cart. We can complete our purchase without a word, that is, without any direct intervention, or we can even leave the place without buying anything. However, it is amazing to observe many of the free visitors in our temple of consumption, surprised, alarmed by the bill resulting from their freely chosen promenade! What will happen? Would they try to find reasons from outside themselves, external factors, as the cause of this unexpected result? It is so "natural" for most of us to look away from the "unpleasant" consequences of our actions. We are always ready to work hard to find factors outside of ourselves and, better, authors other than ourselves as the cause of our misfortune![12]

What actually occurred when our typical buyer was so disturbed at being asked to pay for the shopping cart full of his decisions? Nobody but he alone chose the articles in his cart and nobody even said a word to him about it. Nobody!? And what about the crowd of thoughts entering into his mind all the time, suggesting, whispering, pushing, seducing, stressing, manipulating ...? Rousseau, in his *The Reveries of the Solitary Walker*, told us: "I fled deep into the woods in vain; an importunate crowd followed me everywhere and veiled all of the nature to me" (1992, 119).

Wandering in solitude, yet he was not alone: he was with all the thoughts occupying his mind, all the thoughts coming and fading, encouraging or frightening, while every one of them pretended in its turn to be the genuine one, the one to succeed in making him act. To be free requires us to be alert to what is going on, not only around us, but essentially in our minds. Are the thoughts that come to us clear concepts or not? Are they the thoughts that embody our deliberate aims or not? Am I present or not? To be free means I am present in my mind, attentive to my senses, and conscious of the acquired knowledge I mobilize – in discerning, evaluating, and deciding – knowledge that has to be tested in experience and readjusted afterwards. Much of the time we are unaware, absent-minded, at the mercy of shallow, seductive thoughts wrapped up attractively, speaking directly to some of our deficiencies as "trivial faults."

Experiencing leisure can be an excellent way of training ourselves. Free of stress, looking at the wide horizon of possible realizations, I need to ask myself, "What are the thoughts that accompany my reflection, enter into my decision, influence my observations?" I have to check whether the various suggestions fit with my main project: to express and realize my authentic self, my individuality. Looking behind the scenes, before the selected idea becomes an act, I can detect if this future action will enrich my inner self, will empower my capacity to be whomever I aspire to be.

Nevertheless, we must try not to fall into our old trap of dividing life into separate and impermeable parts. We are one, and our life is one whole of existence. Leisure time is an integral part of our total time, where every part of our life, every activity, every understanding realized must be in touch with every other. Coming back from my leisure involvements I can and I am obliged to use all their privileged acquisitions, when I come back to my ordinary activities, at work, at home, and in any other space in which I am submerged. Not only the river of Heraclitus changes each time one enters it, but the one who enters is changed too. In each immersion into the river of life, I discover another facet of myself, another tendency, another sensitivity, which will be with me in the next immersion. The ongoing experience of leisure brings me the invaluable opportunity to serenely be myself, to be the main criterion of my commitment to life. Being myself in leisure space, expressing my substantial freedom, inspired by the distinctive and unique person I aim to be, I do not forget all that and come back to my social and professional life as I was. I return to what is called active life not as I had been but as I have become.

Having experienced being myself and conscious of my essential freedom, which implies my responsibility to myself, I begin to forge my assigned role in every context and am no longer a passive instrument of society.

CONCLUSION: LEISURE, FREEDOM AS A REALM OF INDIVIDUALITY

Recall that life was given to us, but our relationship to life has to be created.[13] This will not be an easy mission if we keep in

mind that we are in a "generalized process of deinstitutionaliza-
tion and interconnection, of traffic and weakened attachment
to territory, organizing new frames of social, cultural and individual life" (Lipovetsky and Serroy 2008, 35). Yet, how many
opportunities exist! To live our life implies discovering its deep
meaning, thanks to the rich and freely adopted links we maintain with it, links including all the aspects and essences of the
world with which we communicate. This is my liberty; this is my
responsibility.

González Pecotche (1996) adds that time is life, and life is an
infinite field of experience in which we can and must become
our selves; and Buber (1955), that our lives are a personal and
individual trajectory enriched by vital dialogue. To undertake
this process of enriching ourselves demands that we start from
a profound base, knowing who we are, what our resources are,
and which deficiencies threaten to impede our efforts to achieve
freedom and realize what we aspire to be. We have to know that
life moves on and doesn't wait: we can conceive our own path
or allow ourselves to be put in orbit; we can be ourselves or be
reduced to a relative and dependent existence.

There is the primordial alternative for those who have
decided to accept freedom instead of suffering it. This implies
they must be aware of their uniqueness and their responsibility
while they invest all their efforts in being who they have to be,
with humility, and with integrity: to see their smallness within
the immensity of life but also their potential greatness, which
first buds and blossoms in an awakened conscience. I have to
concentrate all my energies to be able to realize my encounter
with myself without falling into the trap of narcissistic individualism. "What is the oeuvre of the human oeuvres – for the
interest of life in general – if not the creation by every one of
us, and in ourselves, of a centre absolutely original, where the
universe is reflected in a unique way, impossible to imitate: our
self" (Teilhard de Chardin 1955, 290). The circumstances are
there, our prerogatives also. Leisure space, or better, the serious leisure approach to life, can be a wonderful opportunity
to become worthy of our human prerogatives, to realize our
freedom *for* our self-emancipation.

A human being's hopes, inspired by freedom, tend to breach the rigid patterns that hide the multiplicity of life. Here is the essence of being free, free to come back and begin, to retry and re-begin (Buber 1955). To be free means being able to consider free time an open opportunity to go on towards the wide and infinite horizons before us, and in our inner selves, the fascinating infinity we must explore. With further inquiry, one increases one's ability to understand; by broadening one's perspective, one increases one's ability to know. Through conscience, in a remarkable process of self-improvement we gradually develop the small sanctuary of our humanity, in which our power accumulates and the strength of this home and fortress is built. Into this fortress, no one else can penetrate, even with the removal of all the barriers between ourselves and life.

Experiencing the conquest of freedom we remember that every human process of value is first and foremost a personal process. We note once again that people will always be the sum of the thoughts that reside and act in their inner selves (González Pecotche 1998, 329), the thoughts that they knew to choose, the thoughts that they succeeded in creating and the harmony that they themselves are continually achieving. Their free and open minds are the sanctuary from which they will come forth in their ever new and more aware departure to meet the world and manage their free struggle for life,[14] and to which they will return. They will find it as they left it, either abandoned and alienated due to the great number of invaders (our social identity) who have come and gone as if they belonged there, or preserved and cared for as an essential, heavenly lot. You will not find your selfhood in the mirror provided by others' looks. You discover and recreate you potential individuality with an eye to your inner life, with a serene commitment to your human dignity. Doing so, you sense what it means being free.

While respecting the fact that others are free, we can only invite people not to give up their personal missions, the actualization of their freedom for the discovery and development of their selfhood. "Men are born and remain free" is written in the first article of the "Declaration of the Rights of Man and of the Citizen," a legacy of the French Revolution, but the goal is still

far off until each individual appropriates his or her own prerogative to become free.

Leisure – this extraterritorial and independent space, where
one's security is not endangered[15] – can be used as a self-nursery
of freedom, in which one can play seriously and be free to create
one's major oeuvre: one's self. But what, in detail, is "leisure
space?" This area of life is the subject of the next chapter.

2

Leisure Space: Cradle of the Individuated Person

This chapter examines the nature of the leisure space and how the individual may develop a positive, individuated, personal identity within it. But, since leisure can sometimes be inimical to this development, the chapter will also explore some of the conditions leading in this latter direction. The principle assumption throughout is that leisure and devotee work (described later in this chapter) are the main vehicles by which each person creates and maintains a unique, positive, personal identity. At the centre of this process, we will note, lie the leisure/work activity being pursued and that which makes it appealing, the core activity.

THE LEISURE SPACE

When leisure is conceived of as space, it is commonly considered from one of three definitions: institutional, temporal, and geographic. That is, leisure may be defined and examined as it fits in the social organization of community and society, as it fits in the span of daily, weekly, and annual time, and as it fits in the surrounding environment, whether artificial or natural. Analyses of leisure often proceed from two or, at times, all three of these definitions; but to highlight their distinctive features, they will be treated separately here.

Institutional Space

When leisure is conceived of as an institution (e.g., Kaplan 1975, 28–31; Rojek 2000), the thought immediately evokes a tendency to see it in relation to the other institutions of society. That is, by noting that leisure is an institution it is said that leisure is not, for example, family, economy, polity, education, religion, health, or the arts. The institution of leisure intersects in diverse ways with all these other institutions, and others not mentioned, but the position taken in this book is that it is nonetheless its own structural entity. Historically, at least, this stance on the leisure institution was not in vogue. Kelly (1987, 141) describes how sociological research in the past (largely in North America) treated leisure as an institution secondary to the economy (primarily offering recuperation after work) and to the family, as a mechanism for generating solidarity there.

A standard sociological definition of a social institution is that it is a relatively stable set of abstract relationships, patterns of behaviour, roles, norms, and values that emerge as solutions to certain problems of collective living. The collective problem around which leisure has institutionalized is that of how, according to a society's norms and values, people in it use their free time effectively and acceptably.

There exist numerous patterns of leisure behaviour and the motivation associated with particular leisure activities as pursued by different segments of the population. These include stamp collecting, playing chess, watching television, going to the movies, and attending cocktail parties. Baseball games, electronic games, the amateur theatre, the racetrack, the ski slopes – all part of leisure. There are also many abstract relationships within leisure, as exemplified in the relationship between amateur actors and the director of a theatre company. At the group level, there are relationships among clubs, associations, centres, and the like. Furthermore leisure roles are in evidence everywhere (in theatres, in hockey arenas, on trout streams, on ski slopes, over chessboards, in front of television sets). Three of the main values of leisure are the desire for pleasure (hedonism), the desire for variety in the experiences from which pleasure is derived, and the desire to choose one's leisure.

There are two other angles from which to view leisure in institutional space: through leisure in historical perspective and through leisure as a distinctive domain of activities. Historically leisure has varied immensely over the ages as Cross (1990) has observed, over a span of time starting in 1600. Gelber (1999) has discussed the changing nature of hobbies in the United States running from the nineteenth to the first half of the twentieth century. And Stebbins (2009, 29–33) has briefly described leisure as experienced in subsistence societies, classical Greece, and the Judeo-Christian era of the Middle Ages.

At the activity level, all of everyday life may be conceptualized as being experienced in one of three domains: work, leisure, and non-work obligation. Work, says Applebaum (1992, x), has no satisfactory definition, since the idea relates to all human activities. That caveat aside, he sees work, among other ways, as performance of useful activity (making things, performing services) done as all or part of sustaining life, as a livelihood. Some people are remunerated for their work, whereas others get paid in kind or directly keep body and soul together with the fruits of their labour (e.g., subsistence farming, hunting, and fishing).

Stebbins (2009, 24–6) holds that non-work obligation is a terribly understudied area of everyday life (much of it falls under the heading of family and/or domestic life, while obligatory communal involvements are also possible). It consists of the many disagreeable activities engaged in beyond those experienced while pursuing a livelihood, some of which may even be individuating (e.g., getting a distinguishing tattoo, having one's nose pierced for placing a unique ring). Sometimes they are seriously misunderstood, as in coerced "volunteering." But, however they are interpreted, they are capable of undermining positiveness in life, which is most often experienced in leisure.

So the leisure domain stands in considerable contrast to these two obligatory realms of life. Leisure may be defined as: uncoerced activity engaged in during free time, which people want to do and, in either a satisfying or a fulfilling way (or both), use their abilities and resources to succeed at this (Stebbins 2005a). This is an experiential definition (Mannell 1999) – it is based on the experience of leisure – but also one that is both institutional (stressing activities) and temporal (stressing free time). It is, furthermore, the definition on which this book is based.

Temporal Space

It is also possible to look on leisure as free time, as time away from all disagreeable obligations. Nevertheless most scholars guided by the temporal approach see leisure time more narrowly: as that time not spent making a living. This conceptualization, however, fails to cover the non-work obligations mentioned above. Time-use studies, which examine the proportions of time spent at leisure vis-à-vis work, exemplify well this narrower temporal definition of leisure (e.g., Robinson and Godbey 1997; Cushman, Veal, and Zuzanek 2005). Variations in the proportion of time spent at work and away from it in different countries and different parts of the population within countries are among the most intensely scrutinized subjects in leisure studies.

Temporal space may be further understood in terms of "discretionary time commitment" (Stebbins 2006b). This kind of commitment refers to the non-coerced, allocation of a certain number of minutes, hours, days, or other measure of time that a person devotes, or would like to devote, to carrying out an activity. Such commitment is both process and product. That is, people either set (process) their own time commitments (products) or willingly accept such commitments (i.e., agreeable obligations) set for them by others. It follows that disagreeable obligations, which are invariably forced on people by others or by circumstances, fail to constitute discretionary time commitments. In short, discretionary time commitment finds expression in leisure and in the agreeable sides of work

One main problem inherent in this conceptualization of space, whether narrowed to include only work or broadened to include non-work obligations, is that people may be bored during their free time. Boredom can result from inactivity ("nothing to do") or from activity, which alas, has become uninteresting, unstimulating (a common lament about some entertainment television). The same can, of course, happen at work and in obligated non-work settings. Since boredom is a decidedly negative state of mind, it may be argued, following the definition just presented, that logically it is not leisure at all (Stebbins 2003). For leisure is typically conceived of as a positive state of mind, composed of, among other sentiments, pleasant expectations and recollections of activities and situations (Kaplan 1960, 22–5). But it may happen that leisure expectations turn out to be unrealistic, and we get bored (or perhaps angry, frightened, or embarrassed) with the activity in question, transforming it in our view into something quite other than leisure. And all this may occur in free time, which exemplifies well how such time covers a broader area of life than leisure does, which is nested within it.

Comments so far have centred primarily on individuals and their dislike for boredom as coerced, unpleasant obligation. Still, this emotional state, it should be noted, can also have far-reaching personal and social consequences, some of them positive, some of them negative. Cohen-Gewerc (2001) argues that boredom can become a gateway for creative leisure. Individually, it can stimulate people to discover their inner selves, and thereby emancipate themselves from boring tasks and roles. Collectively, widespread boredom in a given group or population can spawn significant social change. William Ralph Inge, twentieth-century British churchman, wrote that "the effect of boredom on a large scale in history is underestimated. It is a main cause of revolutions, and would soon bring to an end all the static Utopias and the farmyard civilization of the Fabians." It is not just that people dislike being bored, but also that they sometimes get angry with their condition and seek to shape the world such that they can escape it (and perhaps punish those felt to have caused it). Most generally put boredom can be an incentive to action to alleviate it.

Geographic Space

Leisure space conceived of in geographic terms refers to the places where leisure activities are pursued. These places may be natural or artificial or a combination of both. Nowadays they may be virtual. Natural spaces include largely unmodified aspects of public and private land, waterways, waterfronts, lakes and oceans, and the air above the earth. True, any of these spaces may be polluted and, as such, modified. But modification of this sort does not make them artificial.

The artificial spaces are built by humans. They include indoor and outdoor swimming pools, basketball courts, and ice rinks. All manner of productions and displays in the fine and entertainment arts occur in circumstances completely or substantially artificial (including symphonic concerts by the lake or the sea or in the mountains). Then there is the built environment that is the shopping mall, strip, or street that is patronized as casual leisure in the form of browsing and the possibility of buying something for the fun of it.

David Crouch (2006) adds to this statement on the scope of geographic space two other "components" (our term). One is virtual space, or cyberspace, which is artificial, too, having an unfathomable vastness shared only with the natural space beyond Earth. The other component – the body – is natural, and of all the geographic spaces, is possibly the one most given to evaluation and signification by the individual and others.

Crouch summarizes the importance of understanding leisure in terms of geographic space:

> Leisure happens, is produced in spaces. These spaces may be material, and related to concrete locations. Yet the spaces, and therefore geographies, of leisure may be metaphorical, even imaginative. Imaginative spaces are not merely in the virtual space of contemporary nature but also in the imagination of [the] consumer and the representations of the agencies providing ... leisure sites: visual culture and other narratives of communication ... Space, then, can be important in metaphorically "shaping," contextualizing leisure and commercial and public policy prefiguring of the meaning of leisure sites, and the leisure experience may be transformed by the way in which individuals encounter those spaces and activities. (2006, 127)

In the language of this book leisure activities also occur in geographic space as just described, which helps shape those activities and give them meaning for the individual participant.

THE CENTRALITY OF ACTIVITY

An activity is a type of pursuit, wherein participants in it mentally or physically (often both) think or do something, motivated by the hope of achieving a desired end. Life is filled with activities, both pleasant and unpleasant: sleeping, mowing the lawn, taking the train to work, having a tooth filled, eating lunch, playing tennis matches, running a meeting, and on and on. Activities, as this list illustrates, may be categorized as work, leisure, or nonwork obligation. They are, furthermore, general. In some instances they refer to the behavioural side of recognizable roles, for example commuter, tennis player, and chair of a meeting. In others we may recognize the activity but not conceive of it so formally as a role, exemplified in someone sleeping, mowing a lawn, or eating lunch (not as patron in a restaurant).

This definition of activity gets further refined in the concept of core activity: a distinctive set of interrelated actions or steps that must be followed to achieve the outcome or product that the participant seeks. As with general activities core activities are pursued in work, leisure, and non-work obligation. Consider some examples in serious leisure: a core activity of alpine skiing is descending snow-covered slopes; in cabinet making, it is shaping and finishing wood; and in volunteer firefighting, it is putting out blazes and rescuing people from them. In each case, the participant takes several interrelated steps to successfully ski downhill, make a cabinet, or rescue someone. In casual leisure, core activities – which are much less complex than in serious leisure – are exemplified in the actions required to hold sociable conversations with friends, savour beautiful scenery, and offer simple volunteer services (e.g., handing out leaflets, directing traffic in a theatre parking lot, clearing snow off the neighbourhood hockey rink). Work-related core activities are seen in, for instance, the actions of a surgeon during an operation or the improvisations on a melody by a jazz clarinettist. The core activity in mowing a lawn (non-work obligation) is pushing or riding the mower. Executing an attractive core activity and its component steps and actions is the main feature drawing participants to the general activity encompassing it, because this core directly enables them to reach a cherished goal. It is the opposite for disagreeable core activities. In short the core activity has motivational value of its own, even if more strongly held for some activities than others and even if some activities are disagreeable but still have to be done.

Core activities can be classified as simple or complex, the two concepts finding their place at opposite poles of a continuum. The location of a core activity on this continuum partially explains its appeal or lack thereof. Most casual leisure is comprised of a set of simple core activities. Here *Homo otiosus* (leisure man) need only turn on the television set, observe the scenery, drink the glass of wine (no oenophile is he), or gossip about someone. Complexity in casual leisure increases slightly when playing a board game using dice, participating in a Hash House Harrier treasure hunt, or serving as a casual volunteer by, say, collecting bottles for the Scouts or making tea and coffee after a religious service. And Harrison's (2001) study of upper-middle-class Canadian mass tourists revealed a certain level of complexity in their sensual experience of the touristic sites they visited. For people craving the simple things in life, this is the kind of leisure to head for. The other two domains abound with equivalent simple core activities, as in the work of a parking lot attendant (receiving cash/making change) or the efforts of a householder whose non-work obligation of the day is raking leaves.

So, if complexity is what people want, they must look elsewhere. Leisure projects are necessarily more complex than casual leisure activities. The types of projects listed later in this chapter provide, I believe, ample proof of that. Nonetheless, they are not nearly as complex as the core activities around which serious leisure revolves. The accumulated knowledge, skill, training, and experience of, for instance, the amateur trumpet player, hobbyist stamp collector, and volunteer emergency medical worker are vast, and defy full description of how they are applied during conduct of the core activity. Of course, neophytes in serious leisure activities lack these acquisitions, though it is unquestionably their intention to acquire them to a level where they will feel fulfilled. As with simple core activities complex equivalents also exist in the other two domains. Examples in work include the two earlier examples of the surgeon and jazz clarinettist. In the non-work domain consider two, more or less complex examples: driving in city traffic and (for some people) preparing their annual income tax return.

All this is carried out in the three previously mentioned domains. Because we are concerned in this book with leisure and with work that is essentially leisure, we devote the next two sections of this chapter to the theoretic framework that will frame our discussion of personal development through leisure and the ramifications of such development for the larger community.

THE SERIOUS LEISURE PERSPECTIVE

The serious leisure perspective is a theoretic framework that synthesizes three main forms of leisure, showing, at once, their distinctive features, similarities, and interrelationships (Stebbins 2007). The definition of leisure on which the serious leisure perspective rests is the one set out earlier in the section on leisure space (pp. 29–34). The three forms – serious, casual, and project-based leisure – are briefly defined as follows:

- *Serious leisure* – Systematic pursuit of an amateur, hobbyist, or volunteer activity sufficiently substantial, interesting, and fulfilling for the participant to find a (leisure) career there, acquiring and expressing a combination of its special skills, knowledge, and experience.
- *Casual leisure* – Immediately, intrinsically rewarding, relatively short-lived pleasurable activity, requiring little or no special training to enjoy it. Casual leisure is essentially hedonic.
- *Project-based leisure* – Short-term, reasonably complicated, one-shot or occasional, though infrequent, creative undertaking, carried out in free time, or time free of disagreeable obligations.

Over the years extensive exploratory research and grounded theoretic analysis of data on free-time activity have made it possible to create a typological map of the world of leisure (see figure 1).

That is, so far as can be determined at present, all leisure (at least all leisure in the West) may be classified according to one of these three forms and their several types and subtypes. More

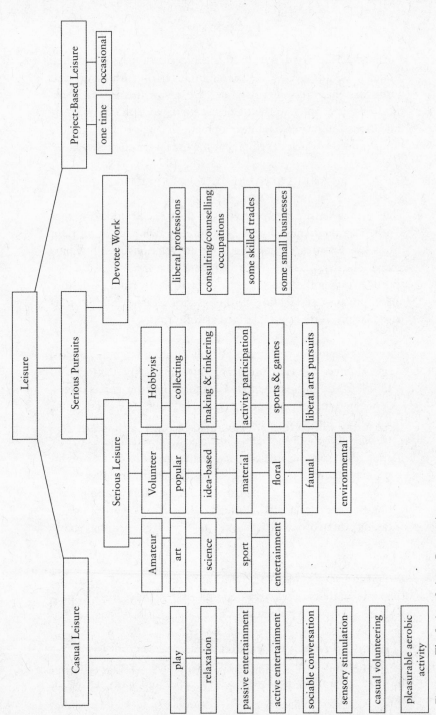

Figure 1 The Serious Leisure Perspective

precisely the serious leisure perspective offers a classification and explanation of all leisure activity and experience, as these two are framed in the social-psychological, social, cultural, and historical contexts in which the activity and experience take place.

Note that this classification has recently been changed (see Stebbins 2012): in figure 1 serious leisure and occupational devotion are now placed under the heading of "Serious Pursuits." The argument supporting this change is set out in Stebbins (2012), justified in general by the observation that devotee work is essentially serious leisure. That making a living by devotee work is a relatively superficial consideration compared with the serious leisure nature of the work activity and the conditions that make it possible.

The body of research supporting the serious leisure perspective is set out in three consecutive summaries (Stebbins 1992, 2001, 2007) and in the continuously updated bibliography in the Serious Leisure Perspective Web site (www.seriousleisure.net). Empirical support is greatest for the propositions bearing on serious leisure. Research guiding those related to casual leisure has been much thinner, while project-based leisure, conceptualized in 2005, has so far led to the fewest studies. Be that as it may, all three forms will be further elaborated below. For the other two forms may have links to serious leisure, mostly notably, however, when a casual or project-based leisure activity becomes the soil in which a career in serious leisure and possibly devotee work takes root (e.g., dabbling on the violin leads to playing it as an amateur and, perhaps later, joining a professional symphony orchestra).

Serious Leisure

It is now time to add to the foregoing definition. Thus amateurs are distinguished from hobbyists by the fact that the former, because they are found in art, science, sport, and entertainment, have a professional counterpart, whereas the latter do not. Some hobbyists, however, have commercial counterparts. Their five types are set out in figure 1. Participants in activities include people who hunt, canoe, gather mushrooms, and watch birds. Hobbyist players of sports and games lack professional counterparts. The liberal arts hobbies are based on self-education in an area of life or literature. Serious leisure volunteers offer uncoerced, altruistic help either formally or informally with no or, at most, token pay and done for the benefit of both other people (beyond the volunteer's family) and the volunteer.

All serious leisure is further defined by six distinguishing qualities (Stebbins 2007). One is the occasional need to persevere, such as in learning how to be a capable museum guide. Yet, it is clear that positive feelings about the activity come, to some extent, from sticking with it through thick and thin, from conquering adversity. A second quality is that of finding a career in the serious leisure role, shaped as it is by its own special contingencies, turning points, and stages of achievement or involvement. Careers in serious leisure commonly rest on a third quality: significant personal effort based on specially acquired knowledge, guidance, experience, or skill, and, indeed, all four at times. Fourth, several durable benefits, or broad outcomes, of serious leisure have so far been identified, mostly from research on amateurs. They are self-development, self-enrichment, self-expression, regeneration or renewal of self, feelings of accomplishment, enhancement of self-image, social interaction and belongingness, and lasting physical products of the activity (e.g., a painting, scientific paper, piece of furniture). A further benefit is that of self-gratification, or the combination of superficial enjoyment and deep fulfillment. Of these benefits, self-fulfillment – realizing, or the fact of having realized, to the fullest one's gifts and character, one's potential – is the most powerful of all.

A fifth quality of serious leisure is the unique ethos that grows up around each instance of it. A central component of this ethos is its special social world in which participants pursue their free-time interests. D.R. Unruh developed the following definition:

> A *social world* must be seen as a unit of social organization which is diffuse and amorphous in character. Generally larger than groups or organizations, social worlds are not necessarily defined by formal boundaries, membership lists, or spatial territory ... A social world must be seen as an internally recognizable constellation of actors, organizations, events,

and practices which have coalesced into a perceived sphere of interest and involvement for participants. Characteristically, a social world lacks a powerful centralized authority structure and is delimited by ... effective communication and not territory nor formal group membership. (1980, 277)

The sixth quality rests on the preceding five: participants in serious leisure tend to identify strongly with their chosen pursuits.

These six qualities have commonly been used to separate serious from casual leisure. This procedure is necessary when studying a leisure activity for the first time, since it is by no means always evident at the start whether it is serious, casual, or project-based. A comparison of serious and casual leisure along the lines of the six qualities is available in Stebbins (2007).

MOTIVATION   Furthermore certain rewards and costs come with pursuing a hobbyist, amateur, or volunteer activity. Both implicitly and explicitly, much of serious leisure theory rests on the following assumption: to understand the meaning of such leisure for those who pursue it is in significant part to understand their motivation for the pursuit. Moreover, one fruitful approach to understanding the motives that lead to serious leisure participation is to study them through the eyes of the participants who, past studies reveal (Stebbins 1992, chap. 6; 1996a; 1998; Arai and Pedlar 1997), see it as a mix of offsetting costs and rewards experienced in the central activity. The rewards of this activity tend to outweigh the costs, however – the result being that the participants usually find a high degree of personal fulfillment in them.

The rewards of a serious leisure pursuit are the more or less routine values that attract and hold its enthusiasts. Every serious leisure career both frames and is framed by the continuous search for these rewards, a search that takes months, and in some fields years, before the participant consistently finds deep satisfaction in his or her amateur, hobbyist, or volunteer role. Ten rewards have so far emerged in the course of my various exploratory studies of amateurs, hobbyists, and career volunteers. As the following list shows, the rewards are predominantly personal.

Personal rewards

1 Personal enrichment (cherished experiences)
2 Self-actualization (developing skills, abilities, knowledge)
3 Self-expression (expressing skills, abilities, knowledge already developed)
4 Self-image (known to others as a particular kind of serious leisure participant)
5 Self-gratification (combination of superficial enjoyment and deep fulfillment)
6 Re-creation (regeneration) of oneself through serious leisure after a day's work
7 Financial return (from a serious leisure activity)

Social rewards

8 Social attraction (associating with other serious leisure participants, with clients as a volunteer, participating in the social world of the activity)
9 Group accomplishment (group effort in accomplishing a serious leisure project: senses of helping, being needed, being altruistic)
10 Contribution to the maintenance and development of the group (including senses of helping, being needed, being altruistic in making the contribution).

Further, every serious leisure activity contains its own costs – a distinctive combination of tensions, dislikes, and disappointments – which each participant confronts in his or her special way. Tensions and dislikes develop within the activity or through its imperfect mesh with work, family, and other leisure interests. Put more precisely, the goal of gaining fulfillment in serious leisure is the drive to experience the rewards of a given leisure activity, such that its costs are seen by the participant as more or less insignificant by comparison. This is at once the meaning of the activity for the participant and that person's motivation for engaging in it. It is this motivational sense of the concept of reward that distinguishes it from the idea of durable benefit set out earlier, an idea that emphasizes outcomes rather than antecedent conditions.

Nonetheless, the two ideas constitute two sides of the same social-psychological coin. Moreover, this brief discussion shows that some positive psychological states may be founded, to some extent, on particular negative, often noteworthy, conditions (e.g., tennis elbow, frostbite [cross-country skiing], stage fright, frustration [in acquiring a collectable, learning a part]). Such conditions can make the senses of achievement and self-fulfillment even more pronounced as the enthusiast manages to conquer adversity, even if doing so is not "fun."

THRILLS AND PSYCHOLOGICAL FLOW   Thrills are part of this reward system. Thrills, or high points, are the sharply exciting events and occasions that stand out in the minds of those who pursue a kind of serious leisure or devotee work. In general, they tend to be associated with the rewards of self-enrichment and, to a lesser extent, those of self-realization and self-expression. That is, thrills in serious leisure and devotee work may be seen as situated manifestations of certain more abstract rewards; they are what participants in some fields seek as concrete expressions of the rewards they find there. They are important, in substantial part because they motivate the participant to stick with the pursuit in hope of finding similar experiences again and again and because they demonstrate that diligence and commitment may pay off. Because thrills, as defined here, are based on a certain level of mastery of a core activity, they have no equivalent in casual leisure. The thrill of a roller coaster ride is qualitatively different from a successful descent over a roaring rapids in a kayak where the boater has the experience, knowledge, and skill to accomplish this.

Over the years I have identified a number of thrills that come with the serious leisure activities I studied. These thrills are exceptional instances of the flow experience. Thus, although the idea of flow originated with the work of Mihalyi Csikszentmihalyi (1990), and has therefore an intellectual history quite separate from that of serious leisure, it does nevertheless happen, depending on the activity, that it is a key motivational condition there. For example, I found flow was highly prized in the hobbies of kayaking, mountain/ice climbing, and snowboarding (Stebbins 2005b). What then is flow?

The intensity with which some participants approach their leisure suggests that, there, they may at times be in psychological flow. Flow, a form of optimal experience, is possibly the most widely discussed and studied generic intrinsic reward in the psychology of work and leisure. Although many types of work and leisure generate little or no flow for their participants, those that do are found primarily in the "devotee occupations" (discussed later) and serious leisure. Still, it appears that each work and leisure activity capable of producing flow does so in terms unique to it. And it follows that each of these activities, especially their core activities, must be carefully studied to discover the properties contributing to the distinctive flow experience it offers.

In his theory of optimal experience, Csikszentmihalyi (1990, 3–5, 54) describes and explains the psychological foundation of the many flow activities in work and leisure, as exemplified in chess, dancing, surgery, and rock climbing. Flow is "autotelic" experience, or the sensation that comes with the actual enacting of intrinsically rewarding activity. Over the years Csikszentmihalyi (1990, 49–67) has identified and explored eight components of this experience. It is easy to see how this quality of complex core activity, when present, is sufficiently rewarding and, it follows, valued highly enough to endow it with many of the qualities of serious leisure, thereby rendering the work and leisure, at the motivational level, inseparable in several ways. And this holds even though most people tend to think of the two as vastly different. The eight components are:

1 Sense of competence in executing the activity;
2 Requirement of concentration on the activity;
3 Clarity of goals of the activity;
4 Immediate feedback from the activity;
5 Sense of deep, focused involvement in the activity;
6 Sense of control in completing the activity;
7 Loss of self-consciousness during the activity; and
8 Sense of time being truncated during the activity.

These components are self-evident, except possibly for the first and the sixth. With reference to the first, flow fails to develop when the activity is either too easy or too difficult; to experience flow, the participant must feel capable of performing a moderately challenging activity. The sixth component refers to the perceived degree of control the participant has over execution of the activity. This is not a matter of personal competence; rather it is one of degree of manoeuvrability in the fact of uncontrollable external conditions, a condition well-illustrated in situations faced by the mountain hobbyists mentioned above, as when the water level suddenly rises on the river or an unpredicted snowstorm results in a whiteout on a mountain snowboard slope. Viewed from the serious leisure perspective psychological flow tends to be associated with the rewards of self-enrichment and, to a lesser extent, those of self-actualization and self-expression.

Casual Leisure

There are eight types of casual leisure (see figure 1). The last and newest addition to this typology – pleasurable aerobic activity – refers to physical activities that require effort sufficient to cause marked increase in respiration and heart rate. Here reference is to "aerobic activity" in the broad sense, to all activity that calls for such effort. Thus the concept includes the routines pursued collectively in (narrowly conceived of) aerobics classes, those pursued individually by way of televised or videotaped programs of aerobics, and most recently, "exertainment" through physical video games (Stebbins 2004b). Yet, as with its passive and active cousins in entertainment, pleasurable aerobic activity is, at bottom, casual leisure. That is, to do such activity requires little more than minimal skill, knowledge, or experience.

Project-Based Leisure

Whereas systematic exploration may reveal others, two types of project-based leisure have so far been identified: one-off projects and occasional projects.

ONE-OFF PROJECTS   In all these projects people generally use the talents and knowledge they have at hand, even though for some projects they may seek beforehand certain instructions. This may include reading a book or taking a short course. And certain projects may require some preliminary conditioning. Always the goal is to undertake successfully the one-off project and nothing more, and sometimes a small amount of background preparation is necessary for this. It is possible that a survey would show that most project-based leisure is hobbyist in character, while its next most common type is a distinctive kind of volunteering. First, the following hobbyist-like projects have so far been identified:

- Making and tinkering:
  - Interlacing, interlocking, and knot-making from kits
  - Other kit assembly projects (e.g., stereo tuner, craft-store projects)
  - Do-it-yourself projects done primarily for fulfillment, some of which may even be undertaken with minimal skill and knowledge (e.g., building a rock wall or a fence, finishing a room in the basement, planting a special garden). This could turn into an irregular series of such projects, spread over many years. They might even transform the participant into a hobbyist.
- Liberal arts:
  - Genealogy (not as ongoing hobby)
  - Tourism: special trip (not as part of an extensive personal tour program) to visit different parts of a region, a continent, or much of the world
  - Activity participation: long backpacking trip, canoe trip; one-off mountain ascent (e.g., Fuji, Rainier, Kilimanjaro)

One-off volunteering projects are also common, though possibly somewhat less so than hobbyist-like projects. And less common than either are the amateur-like projects, which appear to be concentrated in the sphere of theatre.

- Volunteering:
  - Volunteering at a convention or conference, whether local, national, or international in scope

- Volunteering at a sporting competition, whether local, national, or international in scope
- Volunteering at an arts festival or special exhibition mounted in a museum
- Volunteering to help restore human life or wildlife after a natural or human-made disaster caused by, for instance, a hurricane, earthquake, oil spill, or industrial accident
- Arts projects (this new category replaces and subsumes entertainment theatre; see Stebbins 2011):
  - Entertainment theatre: producing a skit or one-off community pageant; preparing a home film, video, or set of photos
  - Public speaking: preparing a talk for a reunion, an after-dinner speech, an oral position statement on an issue to be discussed at a community meeting
  - Memoirs: therapeutic audio, visual, and written productions by the elderly; life histories and autobiographies (all ages); accounts of personal events (all ages) (Stebbins 2011)

OCCASIONAL PROJECTS Preliminary observation suggests that occasional projects are more likely than their one-off cousins to originate in or be motivated by agreeable obligations. Examples of occasional projects include the sum of the culinary, decorative, or other creative activities undertaken, for example, at home or at work for a religious occasion or someone's birthday. Likewise, national holidays and similar celebrations sometimes inspire individuals to mount occasional projects consisting of an ensemble of inventive elements.

Occupational Devotion

In occupational devotion the line between work and (serious) leisure is virtually erased. Occupational devotion is a strong, positive attachment to a form of self-enhancing work, where the sense of achievement is high and the core activity (set of basic tasks) is endowed with such intense appeal that this work and leisure become virtually one and the same (Stebbins 2004a). This devotion is evident in the actions, lifestyle, motivation, and social relations of the occupational devotee. In working at the core activity devotees realize a unique combination of strongly seated cultural values, among them, success, achievement, freedom of action, individual personality, and activity in the form of their job's core activities. Furthermore they find deep self-fulfillment in their work. Nevertheless devotees are workers earning a livelihood. Others categories of workers may also be animated by some or all of these values and rewards, but fail for various reasons to realize them through employment.

Occupational devotees turn up chiefly, though not exclusively, in four areas of the economy, provided that their work there is, at most, only lightly bureaucratized: certain small businesses, the skilled trades, the consulting and counselling occupations, and the public- and client-centred professions. Devotee small businesses include custom work, animal work, artistic crafts, and planning services. Public-centred professions serve publics found in the arts, sports, scientific, and entertainment fields, whereas those that are client-centred serve clients in such fields as law, medicine, accounting, and engineering (Stebbins 1992).

The fact of devotee work for some people and its possibility for others signals that work, as one of life's domains, can be positive. Granted, most workers are not fortunate enough to find such work. For those who do find it, the work meets six criteria (Stebbins 2004a, 9). To generate occupational devotion:

1 The valued core activity must be profound; to perform it acceptably requires substantial skill, knowledge, or experience or a combination of two or three of these.
2 The core must offer significant variety.
3 The core must also offer significant opportunity for creative or innovative work, as a valued expression of individual personality. The adjectives "creative" and "innovative" stress that the undertaking results in something new or different, showing imagination and application of routine skill or knowledge. That is, boredom is likely to develop only after the onset of fatigue experienced from long hours on the job, a point at which significant creativity and innovation are no longer possible.
4 The would-be devotee must have reasonable control over the amount and disposition of time put into the occupation

(the value of freedom of action), such that he can prevent it from becoming a burden. Medium and large bureaucracies have tended to subvert this criterion. For, in the interest of the survival and the development of their organization, managers have felt they must deny their non-unionized employees this freedom, and condition them to accept stiff deadlines and heavy workloads. But no activity, be it leisure or work, is so appealing that it invites unlimited participation during all waking hours.

5 The would-be devotee must have both an aptitude and a taste for the work in question. This is, in part, a case of one man's meat being another man's poison. John finds great fulfillment in being a physician, an occupation that holds little appeal for Jane who, instead, adores being a lawyer (work John finds unappealing).

6 The devotees must work in a physical and social milieu that encourages them to pursue often and without significant constraint the core activity. This includes avoidance of excessive paperwork, caseloads, class sizes, market demands, and the like.

Sounds ideal, if not idealistic, but in fact occupations and work roles exist that meet these criteria. Nevertheless in today's climate of occupational deskilling, over-bureaucratization, and similar impediments to fulfilling core activity at work, many people find it difficult to locate or arrange devotee employment. The six criteria just listed also characterize serious leisure (see Stebbins 2004a, chap. 4), which gives further substance to the claim put forward in the 2004 book that such leisure and devotee work occupy a great deal of common ground.

BECOMING INDIVIDUATED THROUGH LEISURE

If leisure is the cradle of the individuated person, as the title of this chapter asserts, how in detail does he or she reach this state? We have been able to identify six steps by which leisure leads to individuality. Through this process people become distinctive human beings, enabling them to enjoy a special personal identity within one or more of the social circles in which they participate during their daily and weekly rounds. As earlier our conceptualization of leisure in this progression extends to its close relative, devotee work.

Step 1: Setting Preferences

The first step for the individual is to acquire a set of personal values and tastes that harmonize with that person's capacity and talent for engaging in particular leisure activities. In summative terms these values and tastes are the individual's preferences. It is by way of leisure activities and their core tasks that participants realize a unique combination of, what are for them, strongly held cultural values: success, achievement, freedom of action, individual personality, and activity (being involved in something). Robin Williams (2000, 146), who developed this list, failed to include another value which is critical to this discussion, namely, that of time. The dictum "time is money" attests how much we value time for meeting work and other obligations and, to be sure, for pursing leisure activities. Moreover, when it comes to setting preferences, all these values must be in harmony with a person's deep convictions about life and human beings.

During casual leisure, participants realize fewer of these values than during serious leisure. At times specialized consumption by modern youth does lead to individualization of personality, as through participation in one of the postmodern "tribes" discussed by Maffesoli (1996).[1] To elect for a casual leisure activity does demonstrate one's freedom, and is a way of becoming involved. But to be so involved is not to realize values of success or achievement, and is not to realize one's personal identity, at least not independently of the tribes surrounding such activity.

Although we know of no research actually and directly demonstrating that serious leisure participants believe they have achieved something important and are therefore successful, it seems reasonable to conclude that most would feel precisely this way about these two values. After all, compared with others in their reference groups, they have developed considerable knowledge and skill and acquired a great deal of experience, all of which they have often applied with a certain level of perseverance and creativity or innovation. These two values cannot be realized through casual leisure, and can be realized only in a limited way in many leisure projects (e.g., making and tinkering, entertainment theatre).

Serious leisure and, to a lesser extent, project-based leisure also help their participants realize the value of individual personality. The first type of leisure participants are individuated primarily by their exceptional skill, knowledge, and experience as manifested in the core tasks of the leisure using creativity, innovation, perseverance, and so on. In the second type of leisure, some people are individuated through their identity as participants in certain prestigious projects (e.g., in a well-known art or sport event, a celebrated festival, museum, or community event). Additionally some constructed leisure projects can generate a unique reputation for their creators, as in the seventeen interconnected Watts Towers in Los Angeles, built over thirty-three years by Sabato Rodia, and Gilles Maheux's 110-square-meter fantasy city, built from 1.5 million plastic blocks.

Our values help shape our taste for particular leisure and devotee-work activities, though it is probable that the reverse is also true: taste influences values. Moreover physical capacity, or ability, and native talent for particular activities also influence both taste and values. Knowing well our preferences puts us in good position to take the second step. But be aware that all six steps may influence each other through a feedback loop. For example, developing a certain level of knowledge about how to engage most rewardingly in an activity could possibly increase our taste for it as well as improve our capacity to do it. In other words, the six steps are, in reality, more indistinct – have more overlap – than will be evident from this theoretic statement.

Step 2: Using Agency

Personal agency is the state of being able to put into effect what an individual intends to do. The individual is his own agent in producing the intended outcome. Sometimes personal agency can operate only in collaboration with other people, the intended outcome being dependent on their help. Thus, a concert violinist can only perform her concerto when accompanied by an orchestra guided by its conductor, a quarterback in American football cannot express his agency as a passer unless there is a teammate downfield trying to catch the ball he is passing.

It is through particular activities that people, propelled by their own agency, find positive things in life, which they blend and balance with the negative, or disagreeably obligatory, things they must also deal with. Uncoerced, people in leisure believe they are doing something they are not pushed to do, something they are not disagreeably obliged to do. In this definition, emphasis is ipso facto on the acting individual and self-direction through his personal agency.

Still this in no way denies that there may be things people want to do but cannot do because of any number of constraints on their choice. That is, there are limiting social and personal conditions, for example aptitude, ability, socialized leisure tastes, knowledge of available activities, and accessibility of activities. In other words, when using the definition of leisure set out earlier, whose central ingredient is lack of coercion, we must be sure to understand leisure activities in relation to their larger personal, structural, cultural, and historical background. Hence leisure is not really freely chosen, as some observers have claimed (e.g., Parker 1983, 8–9; Kelly 1990, 7), since choice of activity is significantly shaped by this background.

Step 3: Acquiring the Necessities

In serious leisure and devotee work, being able to carry out the core activity always depends on acquiring relevant skills, knowledge, training, or experience and, commonly, a combination of two or more of these four. This is why step 3 is labelled "Acquiring the Necessities." Casual leisure, by its nature, lacks this condition, while project-based leisure, if it has it, calls for necessities that are much shallower than those found in serious leisure.

The role of self-directed learning looms large here. Even in devotee work participants acquire a great deal by way of this process. Roberson (2005, 205) notes the crucial differences between adult education and self-directed learning and then links the second to serious leisure. Drawing on an earlier conceptualization by Lambdin (1997), he says that "self-directed learning is intentional and self-planned learning where the individual is clearly in control of this process." Such learning may be formal (here it is synonymous with adult education), but more often, it is informal. An important condition is that the learner controls the start, direction, and termination of the learning experience (uses agency). Both adult education and self-directed learning are types of "lifelong learning." The latter is a broader idea than the first two, summarized by Selman and colleagues (1998, 21) as learning done throughout a person's lifetime, "from the cradle to the grave." In our book we will show how leisure can provide this lifelong learning with a large focus on the inner self.

Step 4: Finding Fulfillment

Self-fulfillment is either the act or the process of developing to the full one's capacity, more particularly, developing one's gifts and character. Pursuing a fulfilling activity leads to self-fulfillment, although experiencing this condition takes time. This is step 4, which rests on the necessities acquired in step 3. It takes substantial amounts of the relevant skills, knowledge, training, and experience to reach fulfillment in the activity to which they apply. These acquisitions often take years to develop, which is why the idea of formative career is so central.

A formative career is the individual's sense of continuous, positive personal development as it unfolds over the years (Stebbins 2009, 68–9). Two major components of the formative career are the leisure career and that of devotee work. Of these two the first is the more foundational, since a large majority of today's devotee occupations actually owe their existence, in one way or another, to one or more serious leisure precursors (Stebbins 2004a, 73–5).

A leisure career is the typical course, or passage, of a type of amateur, hobbyist, or volunteer that carries the person into and through a leisure role and possibly into and through a (usually devotee) work role. The effect of human agency on a person's career in serious leisure, and possibly later in occupational devotion, is evident in his or her acquisition and expression of a combination of the special skills, knowledge, and experience associated with the core activities. Furthermore every serious leisure career both frames and is framed by the continuous search for certain rewards, a search that takes months, and in some fields years, before the participant consistently finds deep fulfillment in the chosen amateur, hobbyist, or volunteer role or sometimes later on, in a variety of devotee work. A leisure career thus requires a major source of motivation to continue pursuing the activity. Moreover, the essence of any career, whether in work, leisure, or elsewhere, lies in the temporal continuity of the events and activities associated with it.

Step 5: Maintaining Authenticity

Snyder and Lopez (2007, 241), who see authenticity as an important aspect of positive psychology, define the first as follows: "acknowledging and representing one's true self, values, beliefs, and behaviors to oneself and others." Stated otherwise being authentic means being honest with oneself and with one's presentation of self to others. This is step 5 in becoming an individual through leisure. Charles Taylor (1991, chap. 3) adds that being true to ourselves is a "powerful moral ideal." It is a form of personal sincerity.

Still we must nuance Taylor's observation by noting that the definition of authenticity just presented is free of the connotation of moral correctness that is sometimes said to go with this trait. To be precise, some people are quite capable of being authentically deviant, of openly admitting that, for example, they are members of an aberrant religious group, patronize a local nudist resort, or believe unidentified flying objects are operated by alien beings. Tolerable deviance (Stebbins 1996b) – of which these three are instances, though morally wrong in the larger community – is in many societies not so strongly stigmatized there as to force into inauthentic silence those who practice certain varieties of it.

People seem to find the condition of inauthenticity constraining and consequently disagreeable. By the same token they find, most attractive, those situations where they "can let their hair down" or "be themselves"; these give a positive face to their existence. In this regard Silverberg (2008) learned in a study of a Canadian energy company that one of several reasons its employees gave for liking the firm was that they could be themselves. No posturing required in their work setting, quite unlike some others they had experienced.

Authenticity grows from realistic assessments of self and related achievements. In part this happens when – using skill, knowledge, and experience – we compare ourselves with others pursuing the same activity. A kind of informal, personal ranking of self and those others is thereby reached, as reflected in the social mirror into which each individual looks to see how he or she is viewed by those others. The authentic person accepts this reflected social assessment as reasonably accurate. Thus a runner fond of participating in marathons who consistently places between the eightieth and ninetieth percentile of all contestants, if authentic, might say something on the order of "I am a good marathoner," but could not realistically say "I am a champion marathoner" (i.e., consistently placing among the top four participants in each race entered). Given this record other runners who know this one would tend to describe this person in similar terms.

Step 6: Finding an Individuated Identity

Authenticity comes to the individual by way of personal development, by way of finding fulfillment in the acquisition and expression of special skills, and the like while pursuing over time a serious leisure or devotee work activity. This, in turn, becomes the foundation for a positive personal and social identity. J.R. Kelly explains how this works:

The point is that we are continually learning and relearning who we are. In one episode presentation may be affirmed and a self-image strengthened. In another the response may

be disconfirming and require us either to explain it away
or to revise our personal identity. Especially in our younger
years, the self that we imagine ourselves to be is likely to be
assaulted by the responses of others who reject our portrayal
through scorn, neglect, or derision. We discover in time who
we are and some of the limits of what we may become in the
process of social interaction. (1987, 101)

Achievements in work or leisure that the individual can be proud
of, and can therefore identify with, are themselves real and genuine features of that person's formative career. And, in line with
what we said in step 1, these achievements must also be in harmony with that person's deep convictions about life and human
beings. It follows that most people would like to see themselves
in such terms (personal identity) and present themselves to, and
be seen by, others in a similar light (social identity). There is considerable research to support the proposition that serious leisure
begets a distinctive positive social and personal identity (e.g.,
Green and Jones 2005; Hunt 2008; Higham and Hinch 2009).

Note, however, that personal and social identities are not
necessarily individuated. Indeed one of our theses in this book
is that often they are not individuated. Both types of identity
are founded on the ways people in a society learn to categorize
themselves according to criteria they have gained through socialization while living in that society. Individuation roots in these
categorizations but goes further to bring out the distinctiveness
of a person's social and personal identity, this being the most profound transformation when based on achievements in devotee
work and serious leisure.

Casual leisure is usually too fleeting, mundane, and commonplace for most people to find a distinctive personal identity there.
Watching television, going for a walk, gossiping during sociable conversation, and so on, do not require the necessities (Step
3) or allow for the self-fulfillment (Step 4) on which distinctive
identities are founded. The same may be said for many unskilled
occupations. Nonetheless Hutchinson and Kleiber (2005) found
that casual leisure can serve to restore or affirm valued self-
perceptions when people are faced with stressful life changes.

Here individuals may see themselves as competent and caring, as they work with friends or relatives to help them by way of casual leisure activities to adjust to severe illness or accident.

Project-based leisure may also generate a special personal identity for the individual participant. This identity is not, however, ordinarily based on the necessities set out in step 3. Yet, uncommonly it appears, such leisure may become the occasion for expressing skill and knowledge, whether gained at work or in serious leisure. As an example consider the woman who is renowned in her social circle for baking fine desserts, and who is invited by a friend to provide a selection of them at her son's wedding dinner. This is not the usual way this woman pursues this hobby – the wedding dinner is for her a special project. Nevertheless all six of the antecedent steps have been taken in acquiring this project-based leisure identity. Projects resulting in individuation by way of conspicuous consumption (see chapter 4) offer another route to personal distinctiveness.

UNDERMINING THE QUEST FOR INDIVIDUALITY

Conditions exist that can undermine or stall the acquisition of individuality when searching for it through leisure or devotee work. They are, in effect, negative forces in this otherwise positive experience. Four of them are covered in this section, in which we make no claim to mounting an exhaustive review of all such conditions. The goal is to expand on the observation that developing an identity is not as easy as the preceding six steps might suggest. In fact many people never achieve distinctive identities of the kind discussed here. In this section we examine the undermining conditions of casual leisure, reduction of personal agency, selfishness, and conceit.

Casual Leisure

This form of leisure, as noted earlier, is essentially hedonic. As a result casual leisure, like serious leisure, has its costs, albeit not always the same ones. Some costs occur because the potential benefits of casual leisure have not been realized. Four others have so far been identified, one of which has already been discussed, namely, boredom.

A second cost is that casual leisure is in most instances incapable of producing a distinctive leisure identity for its enthusiasts. Few people are going to proclaim to the world that they are, for example, inveterate nappers, television watchers, or consumers of fast food. To the extent that faceless casual leisure dominates the free time of people, this less than optimal balance of leisure activities deprives them of one or more leisure identities which they could otherwise have. For instance, Roberts (1997, 9–13), after analyzing the literature in the area concluded, notwithstanding arguments to the contrary, that today's evanescent youth scenes fail to offer special identities to those who frequent them. Leisure of the kind found in these scenes can enhance self-confidence and help foster positive self-images, but it is too superficial and transient to generate a special identity.

This situation also suggests a third cost: large blocks of casual leisure, even if not boring, leave little time for serious leisure and therefore, in yet another way, deprive the person of an optimal leisure lifestyle. Also at issue here is a significant reduction in, or at least significant barrier to the rise of, well-being and quality of life. The exclusive or nearly exclusive pursuit of pure pleasure, of hedonism, may bring a certain level of happiness in the form of pleasure, but it can never bring the richest and most enduring expression of that emotion. Schopenhauer commented on happiness and casual leisure on at least one occasion. He observed that "the most general survey shows us that the two foes of human happiness are pain and boredom" (*Personality* [1893] 2007, 25).

A fourth cost of casual leisure is that, most often, it makes only a limited contribution to self and community. Unless a person has through play created or discovered something new, casual leisure is unlikely to produce a distinctive identity. This is one aspect of the fourth cost. Other aspects include the common failure of casual leisure to generate good feelings about oneself (the value of self-esteem) and to lead to self-development (the value of personal improvement). Further, much of casual leisure, beyond its oftentimes substantial economic punch, contributes little to the development of the community, viewed here as participation by its members in an activity resulting in improvement of one or more of its identifiable aspects (Pedlar 1996), and strengthening communal patterns of human and institutional interrelationships (Ploch 1976, 8). Of note, however, are the casual leisure volunteers; they are exceptions to the observations just made, for their work does contribute to self and community (Stebbins 1996c).

Reduction of Personal Agency

Whereas casual leisure does have its costs, it also has some clear benefits. Since a number of these are covered in Stebbins (2007, 41–3), they will not be reviewed here. Meanwhile a benefit not treated there, which bears on the present discussion, emanates from the play type of casual leisure (see figure 1).

Play gives maximal scope to personal agency, far more so than either serious or project-based leisure. If nothing else, activities in these latter two are purposive; in them, there are important goals to be reached. To reach these goals, people must organize their lives and direct their behaviour in ways that further this interest. Not so with play, the activity of players, dabblers, and dilettantes. Following Huizinga's (1955) perspective on play, it may be said that the leisure of such people lacks necessity, obligation, and utility and is produced with a disinterestedness that sets it, as an activity, apart from their ordinary, real lives.

In other words, in serious and project-based leisure – and we must add devotee work to this discussion – there is noticeable room for personal agency, even while the latter is constrained by the purposiveness of such activities. And, to the extent that agency facilitates development of the unique individual, it is constrained here as well. Step 2 is a precondition of the remaining four steps, but it functions in this way at a cost. Yet, if all people did was play and in the course of it exercise maximal agency, they would miss taking the other steps leading to distinctive individuality.

Selfishness

Selfishness is the act of a self-seeker judged as selfish by the victim of that act (Stebbins 1981). When we define an act as selfish, we make an imputation. This imputation is most commonly hurled at perceived self-seekers by their victims, where the self-seekers are felt to demonstrate a concern for their own welfare or advantage at the expense of, or in disregard for, those of the victims. The central thread running through the fabric of selfishness is exploitative unfairness – a kind of personal favouritism infecting the everyday affairs of many people in modern society. In comparing the three forms, it is evident that serious leisure is nearly always the most complicated and enduring of them and, for this reason, often takes up much more of a participant's time (Stebbins 1995). Consequently it is much more likely to generate charges of selfishness. For instance some types of serious leisure and even some project-based leisure can only be pursued according to a rigid schedule (e.g., amateur theatrical rehearsals, volunteer guide work at a zoo, volunteer ticket selling at an arts festival), which unlike most casual leisure, allows little room for compromise or manoeuvre. Thus, imputations of selfishness are considerably more likely to arise with regard to the first two.

Furthermore, we can make a similar observation about serious and causal leisure activities that exclude the participant's partner vis-à-vis those that include this person. Logically speaking, it is difficult to complain about someone's selfishness when the would-be complainer also engages in the activity, especially with significant fulfillment. Furthermore, serious leisure, compared with casual leisure, is often more debatable as selfishness, when seen from the standpoints of both the victim and the self-seeker. For serious leisure enthusiasts have at their fingertips as justifications for their actions such venerated ideals as self-enrichment, self-expression, self-actualization, service to others, contribution to group effort, development of a valued personal identity, and the regeneration of oneself after work. As for casual volunteering it is a partial exception to this observation, in that it, too, can be justified by some of these ideals, most notably volunteer service to others and regeneration of oneself.

Remember the value of individual personality presented above as part of step 1. We value being distinctive persons. Yet, for all but hermits, our distinctiveness must also be favourably viewed by our reference groups and reference others. Acting selfishly toward these people tarnishes the image that most individuals want to see reflected in their evaluation of them. Individuality of the negative kind achieved through selfishness is not what we commonly seek. Meanwhile, positive individuality is undermined by certain significant others who also make demands on that time and money. The latter may conclude sooner or later that the enthusiast is more enamoured of the core leisure activity than of, say, the partner or spouse. Charges of selfishness may then not be far off.

Conceit

Conceit serves to generate negative individuality and undermine positive individuality much the same way as selfishness does. To understand conceit, however, we must consider it in the light of modesty and pride.

Perhaps because it simplifies our cognitive world, we have a tendency to judge all personalities to be modest, proud, or conceited, as if these modes were also traits of character (Stebbins 1972). Valid to some extent, rigid adherence to this image obscures two important points. First, modest, proud, or conceited behaviour is focused; it is enacted with reference to our accomplishments and lines of activity regarded by us and certain others present in the situation, as major forms of positive self-identification. For example, a person might speak proudly of an accomplishment before one group of people and modestly of it before another. Second, some achievements, because of their obvious mediocrity, constitute an insufficient foundation on which to build self-worth. They fail to qualify as something to be proud of or modest about.

Moreover, people are proud, conceited, or modest before an audience: those present in the situation whose opinions of their behaviour there they value. Clearly, there are two viewpoints from which to identify behaviour as typical of one of these three modes: what the individual intends and what the audience perceives. In many instances – perhaps most – individual and audience seem to agree on their definition of the situation, what someone intends as modest discourse, for example, is perceived as such by the audience. But it is also possible, especially with conceit, that there will be occasional discrepancies between what a person intends and what the audience perceives.

The essence of each mode lies in its pointed reference to the speaker; people express their feelings about their own accomplishments. That is, it is reasonable to differentiate verbal modesty, pride, and conceit by amount and kind of discourse about the strengths and weaknesses of an individual's achievements and by amount and kind of discourse about the strengths and weaknesses of the related achievements of others. Thus talk about personal accomplishments tends to be comparative, where everyone in the situation contrasts those of the speaker with those of others being referred to.

Regardless of whose view it is, modesty and pride are commonly seen as socially acceptable variations in the form of self-esteem. On one side, modesty is bordered by a form of humility characterized by low personal regard and manifested in debasing references to self. On the other side, pride is bordered by conceit. Both conceit and the self-effacing form of humility may be considered minor forms of deviant behaviour; persons who act this way are so labelled because they have violated the rules of etiquette held for those who engage in talk about self-worth. It is noteworthy that behaviour identified as conceit usually is defined as such only by the audience, since most people, because of the stigma attached to this sort of talk, try to avoid boasting (at least very much) when they believe the audience will perceive their behaviour this way. When boasting (as defined by the audience) does occur, speakers who do it tend to view their utterances as simply a form of pride.

In this manner conceit can undermine the positive side of individual identity. Our interest in this section lies in how conceit can do this in the leisure space. Since the greatest concern about personal accomplishment in free time lies in serious leisure, we should expect it to be the main stage for expressing conceit. Yet, on this stage, the audience finds the conceited individuated person to be disagreeable, which leads them to lower their estimation of him.

CONCLUSION

The foregoing statement on the four undermining conditions shows how fragile the search for and maintenance of a positive individuated identity can be. For these conditions are anything but minor forces in the life of the individual. True, many people do manage to keep the pursuit of casual leisure in balance, find and retain an acceptable level of personal agency, avoid selfishness, and remain modest and proud (depending on social situation) of what they have accomplished. But it is also easy to succumb to irresistible hedonic pleasures that absorb time from more complex leisure and work pursuits (e.g., excessive gambling and drinking, watching television, engaging in social conversations). Personal agency may be undermined by forces beyond our control, as in new, more restrictive policies (e.g., set by the coach, boss, director) or additional paperwork. As for selfishness it has huge appeal. So much so that William Gladstone, once prime minister of the United Kingdom, observed that: "selfishness is the greatest curse of the human race" (from a speech given in Hawarden, 28 May 1890). And, finally, how easy it is to become immodest about one's accomplishments vis-à-vis those of others, thereby drifting from modesty into conceit.

Let these conditions, and possibly others yet to be discovered through research in this area, help guide a person's quest for individuality. Failure to consider them could end in disappointment. That said, we must nuance the claim made in this chapter that play is casual leisure, and that casual leisure is one of the conditions that can undermine or stall acquisition of individuality when someone is searching for it through leisure or devotee work. For play, as the next chapter shows, is complicated in its effects; it, too, can become a font of individuality.

3

Inclination to Play

As he wandered through the station, he reminded himself of who he was supposed to be:

> The effect of being Paul Auster, he had begun to learn, was not altogether unpleasant. Although he still had the same body, the same mind, the same thoughts, he felt as though he had somehow been taken out of himself, as if he no longer had to walk around with the burden of his own consciousness. By a simple trick of the intelligence, a deft little twist of naming, he felt incomparably lighter and freer. At the same time, he knew it was all an illusion. But there was a certain comfort in that. He had not really lost himself; he was merely pretending, and he could return to being Quinn whenever he wished. (Auster 1990, 61)

Paul Auster plays with, and through, his protagonist Daniel Quinn. He discovers and creates numerous "realities" but he knows, all the while, that he has "not really lost himself; he was merely pretending, and he could return to being" Paul Auster "whenever he" wished.

He has in essence this wonderful human prerogative to go farther and farther away from the concrete circumstances in which he dwells. He can observe, think, imagine, and create, endlessly, new and different alternatives. He can sense how he frees himself from the here and now: he is capable of play, that is, of realizing infinite combinations, possibilities, sensations, and approaches, within a privileged and safe space.

Schiller argued that the instinct to play is something inherent to the human condition. "For, to speak out once for all, man only plays when in the full meaning of the word he is a man, and he is only completely a man when he plays" (1909–14, letter 15). Yet what do we really mean when we say "man plays"? That is the basic issue we will attempt to resolve, with its implications in the realm of free time within the context of the new era of leisure[1] and in what this aspect of human nature entails for individualism and individuality.[2]

"All the world's a stage." We can say that "human beings play" all the time, but not every sort of play leads one to be "completely human." Let us see which kinds of play can potentially bring us closer to our selves, and which throw the player off the course of his or her self. We will begin with that foremost arena of life where we have to play established and pre-scripted roles fitting our performance to what is expected of us.

This is not, however, the "magic circle" described by Huizinga (1955). In that circle, real life confers a sort of immunity on players when, released from our designated social roles, we tend to play in an extraterritorial space within life, where ordinary patterns, laws and rules, pressures, threats, and sanctions are made obsolete. Like in the open-ended time of leisure, when we can do something not a task or an obligation, or even do nothing at all, we can choose any activity "unneeded" for day-to-day living, and mostly without instrumental value. We are in the vast realm of freedom (Huizinga 1955).

Playing in life, according to the social games in which we are implanted, or playing on the fringes of canonical life – how are we able to differentiate these domains? Are we living our lives, playing in "the risky / and the beautiful game of life" as in Borges' poem[3] or are we escaping to the fringes of reality? "Play," "game"? Are these two concepts synonymous? It is easier to get clear-cut answers after we've discovered that play, with its "inherent ambiguity and paradoxical nature" (Wragg 2009), has in itself an essential role in human life.

Louis XVI, the king who fell victim to the French Revolution, was required to play his role of king in that troubled period, although his deep desire was to be a locksmith! Where was he playing? Where was he experiencing his ownmost life? It is well-known that Ingres, the neoclassical French painter (eighteenth century) liked playing violin above all else, a narrative that gave rise to the expression *violon d'Ingres* to define a hobby. We can see Ingres as a precursor to serious leisure. Using this concept, before it emerged in the French language, we can say that Louis XVI aspired to have much more leisure to dedicate himself to his violon d'Ingres, that is, aspired to get this time free from his conventional roles, in order to play.

As we have said before, in previous chapters, leisure space invites us to thoroughly review our concepts of life, and one of these concepts is the meaning of our inclination to play.

Let us enter into the various facets of play.

PLAY AS A NECESSITY

Reality is a complex network of conventions and rules which tend to transform this unpredictable free entity, which by convention is called "man," into a nearly predictable actor of the changing "human comedy."

We play our scripts according to our roles in every scene, that is, according to our audience and the extent of our exposure on stage. In other words, we are accustomed to doing what is expected from us and we are controlled for. We are subject to the "school syndrome," where teachers teach and pupils learn, not for the sake of knowing, but only to be able to pass the official tests. Here the game and its play are sterilized, emptied of their vitality, their renewing potentiality.

It's also true that we have little breaks, like a pupil at school, and can, behind the scenes, discard roles. Yet, very soon, behind the scenes, there emerges another one with another script, with different spectators and a different kind of exposure. The game with its domineering tentacles has to continue and one must play it or not be.

It is well-known that one can lose one's social position because one doesn't play in accordance with the game's rules. Subsequently, it may also occur that a man goes from one stage to another, playing his entire life, that is, being his various characters with little or no space for his unknown self, unknown even to him. And what a drama when circumstances push someone off of the stage! What happens to a devoted mother when all her children have quit the nest? What happens when a man or woman becomes this sort of living ghost called a "has-been" once having left his or her role/status/job?

In the game of life, roles and persons become a symbiotic issue[4] reinforced by the human necessity of social identity. Play then will be only small escapades and short distractions using free time and established leisure, mostly casual and provided by the leisure industries (TV, all-inclusive vacations, for example).

PERSONALITY, INDIVIDUALISM, AND PLAY

According to Suetonius, Augustus Caesar, on the day of his death,

> now and then enquired, if there was any disturbance in the town on his account; and calling for a mirror, he ordered his hair to be combed, and his shrunk cheeks to be adjusted. Then asking his friends who were admitted into the room, "Do ye think that I have acted my part on the stage of life well?" he immediately subjoined,

> If all be right, with joy your voices raise,
> In loud applauses to the actor's praise. (n.d., *The Lives of the Twelve Caesars*, XCIX).

If Suetonius is right, Augustus, until his last moments stayed on stage showing his persona, being sure his hair was combed and his face was looking its best. Could we suppose that he also used to enjoy some leisure time, some moments down from the stage, resting from his alert and intense role playing?

We can see in literature, and cinema, how leading politicians are always aware of the acute need for any opportunity to flee their social-position survival games, to relax for a while – at least in order to revive their energies, before returning to the show. Depending on the social image we have to display and maintain during the days occupied in the various scenes, we sense periodically the need to get down from the stage. One opens his tie, another takes her shoes off, all wanting to quit the persona[5] and be somewhere else.

Far, for a while, from our daily roles, we now play not so much to be ourselves – selves whom we rarely really know – but to be another or, more accurately, to be elsewhere and otherwise. Yet it appears generally that it is not so easy to be elsewhere and otherwise: the feeling of emptiness is there, lying in wait for us. How to fill this void? Knowing well this vague malaise, leisure industries are there, aware, and ready to offer suitable occupations and ways to spend any potentially burdensome free time and "adequate" free money.

DISTRACTION

We need entertainment. This means that we need to be provided with things to fill this time, and this filling has to be the opposite of normal, everyday life, opposite of obligations of any kind – the other part of life. Here we are no longer play-acting; we expect others to play-act for us. We expect to be entertained through having our time, our attention, occupied in any casual leisure. Television with its numerous channels is the main provider of this necessity.

Heirs and heiresses of the long Judeo-Christian tradition (which divides time in two, sacred and secular), we tend to divide life into ordinary days and holidays, at work and on vacation, occupied actively and passively, engaged in meeting obligations and in pursuing distractions. Russell wrote, "since men will not be tired in their spare time, they will not demand only such amusements as are passive and vapid."[6] Nevertheless, we argue that even if being tired is not a basic condition, this advice is insufficient: people need also to be trained to use *their* time, all of their time as a whole. Being aware that time is the basic resource of human life, they will indeed have the opportunity of managing every day, and even every hour, as means to the realization of their goals, that is, of their self-realization. However, people may be easily tempted to consider free time, their free time, only through consumption's prism, promoting our narcissistic individualism in an intensive advertising/harassment for consumption of amusements and excitements whose dosage must be more and more intense to attain any effect.

We can observe this phenomenon in the case of TV programs, the most popular forms of distraction. The dosage of sensationalism, violence, speed, hilarity, and so on increases in all kinds of programs from one season to the next, essentially in those destined for prime time, that is, when the advertising cost is the highest. Even news becomes more and more of an exciting show, with all the enticing ingredients of any dramatic genre. You cannot produce a "decent" edition of the news without some catastrophe, a truculent scandal, or an emotive event. When local news can't supply the goods, editors can pick up the daily dose of brutality or voyeurism from anywhere across the global village. In an environment saturated with innumerable and ever-present solicitations, external stimuli rapidly lose their effect and need to be "reinforced." The film *A Clockwork Orange* (1971) by Stanley Kubrick, which shocked a whole generation, could be seen now by our young consumers as only mildly entertaining, by contrast to their regular doses of exciting images, intense action, and intrusive violence.

Distraction – i.e., casual leisure – must take us far away from our routine game of life. It must make us sense new experiences, give us a lot of anecdotes to talk about, a lot of nostalgia to awaken forgotten memories. Hebrew has an eloquent expression that literally means "to make/produce life," telling how those moments that differ from the ordinary life game allow us to sense a sort of resurrection, the resurrection of our basic tendency to respond to what attracts, what seduces, what makes us enjoy something in a realm different and free of sanctions. The rhetoric of the self in its individualistic track enhances the legitimacy of having a good time with easy joys.

Looking for fun, for excitement, for immediate contentment thanks to those who play for us, is a "legitimate" rest from being ourselves on stage, playing the stressful roles of life. We even have a "participative-passive" distraction when the public is invited to take part in mass-media productions. For instance, we are requested to determine who is to be eliminated from among contestants in a game show or who is the dancer/singer to win the local TV singing or dancing contest. Acting anonymously by phone or by cellular text message enhances self-excitement. These passive participants imagine that they have some influence upon the exciting event produced "for them." They will be happy to tell everyone that their candidate won! These sensational new gimmicks can attract many people all at once, if we engage them using a social network such Twitter or Facebook.[7]

Distraction then becomes active. Playing bridge with partners is for the participants, an important background of their vitality, freed from obligatory roles and playing now in a voluntary activity. We understand that leisure space offers, not only the basic occasion to enjoy physically needed rest, but innumerable occasions to choose free and voluntary activities. You become aware that you really rest, not by being passive, but by changing your activities, quitting the stage where the screenplay is mostly imposed and entering into the scene where you are not only an actor but also at least a partner in the elaboration of a new common text. Here you are at the threshold of the bountiful realm of serious leisure.

Serious leisure space, when it transcends short and inconsistent breaks, can offer us new possibilities to review the concept of play and rediscover the deeply original inclination to play of our childhood, a form of play that can introduce us to the vast game of life, with its infinite facets and potentialities.

PLAYING TO EXPLORE LIFE

Entering into the game, we have to learn of, and train for, the roles that allow us to secure our social survival and earn a decent place in the world. In this context, playing is "in sum ... a way to rehearse reality" (Beatrice 2009), the reality in which we are immersed, with its texts, its rituals, its scores, and its gestures based on its set of views, beliefs, convictions, and habits. This vital training is at the same time an initiation and an exploration: an initiation for a legitimate entry into the social world, and a first experience of enlarging the known sphere, a valorous exercise of exploration of new zones, new things, new situations.

In this subtle play, we develop at once two sorts of playing skills: aptitudes that lead us into conformism, even in the internalized rules of the life game affecting only one's private life and an intrinsic curiosity that pushes us to discover more and more facets, more and more elements at the edges of conventional reality. Individual walks of life will lead some of us to reinforce the tendency to conform and to do so at such a level that there will no longer be room to be curious and even less so to explore, while others will have a sensitivity to the new and different and keep the desire alive inside themselves to discover ways of maintaining that sensitivity.

The first type of playing skill will naturally be one that blurs differences and will therefore erase almost entirely the contours between the whole of existence and the little world enacted on our daily stage. We will meet, for example, people whose roles become them, and who become their roles. They will go across the various stages and through the various scripts without even changing their clothes, like those famous characters in the *comedia del arte*[8] who were present in every performance, or like the key characters in a popular television series who jump from episode to episode, from film to film, and play as whomever the viewing public expects them to be. In this scenario, the game ceases to be a game and becomes life itself; even more, it becomes the whole of life – we can recognize it, for example, if a schoolteacher is speaking to us in the same voice and with the same attitude as in the classroom.[9]

We must consider, in this same context, the games of a ritual nature established in almost all traditions, either the games whose aim it is to mark any significant transition in a person's life, such as birth, puberty, marriage, graduation, and so on, or those whose aim it is to mark exceptional dates in the annual calendar, such as religious or secular feasts, including the various versions of "carnival," where people are supposed to disguise themselves. Playing a new person – or better said, playing a new role with all the familiar elements, including special costumes – is there to reinforce the fabric of a society (Cossu 2009). An eloquent example of the strength of such patterns may be observed in marriage ceremonies "performed religiously" by young couples, and less young couples who have already cohabited for long years. It's amazing the efforts invested by all the "characters" of this production from the white wedding dress to the last detail in the decoration of the wedding hall. Everyone, from the stars of this premiere to the last extra, is aware that they are acting in an extraordinary scene within the comprehensive play of life.

From the devotee participant in the Catholic Carnival in the last days before Lent to his parallel who wins the disguise award on the day of Jewish Purim for his original performance and creative mask – both know that these extraordinary events/scenes are intrinsic parts of the big human comedy and are there to stress the ordinary roles into which the glamorous bride and the disguise winner have to return.[10] Yet Roger Caillois (1967) pointed out how the feast represents such a paroxism of vitality and differs so strongly from the small worries of daily existence – it appears as another world. Let us call it the Cinderella phenomenon: being a prince/princess for a whole, unique night, where we sense we are sustained and transformed by forces that transcend us and instill some crucial memories within the routine game of our lives. We should not misunderstand and think that all these somehow archaic phenomena ensure, in our new century, social cohesion. None of this prevents, or even slows, the massive spread of narrow and narcissistic individualism. Tocqueville argued that when a citizen realizes the makeup of his small society of family and friends, he will feel disconnected from larger society, and he will abandon it to its fate. What remains of traditions today can also be used separately and in narcissistic ways.

The second type of ability to play maintains a slight distance between a person's life and her role in life. She knows – without being aware of it all the time – that she acts through her role and that she plays a game within its limited space, which is not the whole of "space." Yet, as she walks easily on the quite self-evident stage of her daily life, she also looks beyond. This person is attentive to new hints, aspires to meet new aspects of her immense life, the existence of which she imagines and would be happy to discover. Now we are in the presence of someone who (like our first individual) can play with closed eyes, thanks to her long and repeated rehearsals, but keeps herself alert to the infinite fertile nuances even within the seemingly self-evident reality of her role. Thus, it occurs that seeds lie for years in a desert landscape "waiting" for some rain and when it arrives, these invisible seeds become a flourishing garden and metamorphose the scenery all around!

Thus, two essential attitudes can be taken up towards the future, or in our present domain of play, towards new performances. Those who adopt the first tend to just mechanically repeat the same old role; those who adopt the second see every new performance as a basic platform to enable them to discover more, new elements to the performance, even within the established script and their pre-defined roles. Those with the first type of attitude act with eyes closed and a hibernating mind; those with the second open their eyes to events happening in all directions, appealing to all their mental capacities to decipher the innumerable signs springing up all around them and within their inner selves. Those who adopt the first attitude consider a person's play as part of a closed game; those who adopt the second view playing as an ongoing opportunity to open up, to enlarge, and to enrich their vital experience of life.

And if our postmodern and unstable world makes the first attitude quite impossible, our conformist has found a perfect solution by entering with joy into a very comfortable modular conformism, meaning to flow up into the latest trend, to go on being changed by circumstances that instill their new expectations. He doesn't play; he is shaped by the circumstantial nature of the game.

The second type of attitude is also actively involved in change, yet the individual who has this attitude is open to exploring, to evaluating, and to adapting. This person plays and chooses how and how much to change; she shapes her life through her discoveries, her responsible choices. In her mind, playing is a means to go further, enlarging the limits of the local and particular world within the World.

PLAYING TO EXPLORE THE WORLD

Twenty years ago, a concerned father came to ask me what to do with his problematic son: "I used to buy educational toys such as Lego for my eight-year-old son and I played with him showing him the models he was to build but he never was able to accomplish this task. Instead he played for hours building a lot of other things but never the proposed model!"

This young child had discovered the essence of the game and the soul of play, which is to explore more and more possibilities other than the circumstantial reality of the customary option. Even with a limited set of modular elements, he saw that it was possible to create different shapes and devices, which were as legitimate and plausible as the set model that came within the toy box.

He discovered that reality, any reality, is no more than one among a multitude of options, each tending to impose itself as standard. To play means to try different ways of using elements, energies, surroundings. Don't forget the great impact, even now, of the simple but audacious play of Marcel Duchamp, when in 1917 he displayed an ordinary toilet as a work of art, *Fountain*, in a museum hall. What a scandal! But what a mind-shaker! To be able to see the same thing from another point of view is an unfailing step towards freedom, for freedom is essentially the freedom of mind. To play, exploring new views and new linkages, means to experience freedom, a type of freedom that emancipates us from preconceptions and trains us to enlarge our horizons, that is, to search out new ones.

PLAYING AS EXPERIENCE

We will not refer again to those who are trapped in ritualistic routines. They are collaborating, being used as raw material to embody established views, conventions, and rituals in which "play" is a way to reinforce the fabric of a specific society within a known set of beliefs and views. Playing then means a growing dependence on a closed and particular horizon (Wragg 2009). In one sense, there has been since ancestral eras a brilliant way to domesticate the human innate penchant to play (Cossu 2009). People are allowed to play within the safe boundaries of a known and limited world in the World, changing roles for a while within the limits of rituals and, above all, being protected from uncertainty and from freedom. Playing in these arenas allows us to remain on the surface and continue our addiction to effortlessness (González Pecotche 1962). Acting out social roles, we are distanced from our faculties, our own real memory and responsiveness, and act with a kind of semi-presence, as if in automatic-pilot mode.

We are interested rather in the process of play, where "play" means to experience the adventure of walking outside established tracks, towards open alternatives. First of all we must stress the fact that we are involved in playing, that is, acting in a real "unreal" world that we are able to leave at any time. Having a solid base from which we can venture, and to which we can return, gives us the opportunity to play in alternative fields, to experience ideas, aspirations, and to use talents that are not needed for, and have no relevance in, daily life.

The inclination to play is here no longer devoted to rehearsing our conventional role, or what González Pecotche calls our external personality, i.e., the image through which we obtain our position in the eyes of others, our legitimate existence and social survival. Yet, apart from our daily persona, we play by being attentive to our inner self, with all its unique attributes and its special range of interests. We feel ready to try, to go further in the sole purpose of discovering the world beyond our limited one, and having the opportunity to discern more of the still-unknown aspects of our authentic selves.

Play is then a voluntary activity, as Huizinga wrote, and "marks itself off from the course of the natural processes ... it is free, is in fact freedom" (cited in Hockett 1999, 3): this is not freedom to do and to achieve in order to show, to reinforce one's self-image, but freedom to be entirely whomever you perceive you can be.

Like the little baby who is totally devoted to the discovery of his own body – moving, touching, tasting – we enter into play with the same innocent wish to learn about new horizons, in which we will have the chance to discern some echo of our unrevealed self. Hiking outside of the marked paths we are alert to details around and in our inner self. We note how every tree is unique and we reinforce the sense of our own uniqueness. One plays a musical instrument and senses how one's inner strings resonate in harmony with the notes.

Play is also the realm of sharing with partners, not only the game, but also the human experience freed from economic and social dependence. The game becomes the occasion to meet one's other self and life outside of the prism of narrow interests. Play is then no longer a mere distraction, but a serene enterprise, a solid introduction to serious leisure.

EXPERIENCING PLAY TOWARDS INDIVIDUALITY

Experiencing serious play as part of serious leisure (see "Contemplation as Leisure and Non-leisure," Stebbins 2006a) means to experience what Camus (1962) considered to be our essential kingdom beyond our existential exile, yet without harming our necessary achievements in our still necessary exile. In Camus' short stories each hero lives his "kingdom" in parallel with the exile in which he is immersed, until the crucial point of rupture when the bridge can no longer span the widening gap. Camus, in his proposal for the back cover of *L'Exil et le royaume*, defined these two entities: "kingdom here coincides with a sort of free and naked life into which we should return if we want to be reborn finally. Exile, in its way, shows us the path, on the sole condition that at the same time we know how to refuse servitude and possession" (1962, 2031). Entering into the play world, we get into our individual kingdom beyond the established game of servitude and possession, a world we must explore. This will demand fully opened eyes, looking at life around and within us, experiencing a challenging horizon where the obvious is no longer common currency.

To experience play becomes, then, a tangible process that makes us come back to an existence different from the one we left behind. We are thus at the threshold of a realm that invites us to intensify our relationship with ourselves, "we are asked to see ourselves as an object of knowledge and action, in order to transform ourselves" (Foucault 1984, 56). This can be a decisive crossroads, visible essentially in leisure space – a vital moment, when we perceive a second chance to be who we aspire to be, in other words the chance to go beyond the exile where we are shaped to fit the world in which we live. We enter here into the unexplored territory of our inner kingdom, where we have the opportunity to meet ourselves more deeply and thoroughly than in any social circumstance.

In this serious play, you are no longer directed by external circumstances; on the contrary, you are consciously experiencing your own internal individuality. You experience your unique way of sensing your vision of life, which is at the same time an in-depth search for uniqueness and universality. Alphonse de Lamartine, in his famous poem "L'Isolement," could express his particular and essential feeling and reach the universal core of this emotion, where he wrote: "Un seul être vous manque et tout est dépeuplé" (1920, 13), which means essentially that when you miss just one person, the whole world feels empty. In the privileged free time of leisure we can widen the narrow social concept of "recreation" and go beyond the parochial boundaries of a physical restorative. The issue is not to enhance the divorce between the social game and individual play. The leisure realm allows us to move from one to the other, multiplying solid bridges and consistent ways of enriching each.

Playing, then, becomes a vital re-creation of our selves, a free space full of opportunities for us, as individuals, to learn, train, and improve our uniqueness, our authentic individuality. Conscious of our essential selves, we come back to our daily stage, less dependent on conventional patterns, and better able to contribute and to be present in the human social network. As good actors, we can each bring our inner being into our performances of life. You may remember performances of *Hamlet* by actors who became Hamlet with their own unique selves. Yet *Hamlet* remains always *Hamlet*. The script is the same as written by Shakespeare but, thanks to the specific actor and that actor's tangible, unique presence, we experience the miracle of a revitalized Hamlet. Experiencing the play as the magic workshop of being "me as a whole" will enable each of us to achieve our life roles through and towards our consciousness of our uniqueness.

This can be a great contribution of leisure: to invert the classical formula saying that the "role" makes the individual. In the reciprocity of the game of life and the free play of being, a new reality arises where each person, each individual, animates and makes any role what it should be. We would be realizing in this way the third metamorphosis described by Nietzsche in *Thus Spake Zarathustra*, where the human spirit tends to emerge as a unique individual, beyond social conformism. First, the spirit becomes a camel and carries all commitments with courage and determination towards its own desert. Then the second metamorphosis occurs, where the spirit becomes a lion, a unique spirit that can free itself from the dragon of "you-should." This opens the road to the third metamorphosis, that of becoming a child:

> But tell me, my brethren, what the child can do, which even the lion could not do? Why hath the preying lion still to become a child?
>
> Innocence is the child, and forgetfulness, a new beginning, a game, a Self-rolling wheel, a first movement, a holy Yea.
>
> Aye, for the game of creating, my brethren, there is needed a holy Yea unto life: its own will, willeth now the spirit; his own world winneth the world's outcast. (1896, para. 1, "The Three Metamorphoses")

You arrive at the game of creating, the fundamental prerogative of any individual who emerges from passivity. You are freed from being formed externally by non-essential circumstances, and you decide to preside over the creation of yourself: "If, in all domains, life's triumph is creation, we should suppose that human life has its *raison d'être* in creation which can ... continue throughout life in every man: the creation of one's self by one's self?" (Bergson 1966, 24). This can occur, through the "essential player," in the free and open-ended space of leisure. There, we can, as Bergson puts it, "hear singing in the bottom of our souls, a sort of music sometimes joyful, most of the time dolorous, always original, the uninterrupted melody of our inner life" (1900, 66).

Entering into the serious experience of creation invites us to introduce ourselves into the immense sphere of art and its growing place in the leisure era.

CONCLUSION

Starting with Schiller and the inherent inclination to play, we saw how play is a basic necessity leading us in various directions. We may find in play a closed game, where all the cards of life are stacked. But we may also recognize it as a vast horizon, rich in possible alternatives beyond the established life game.

Learning to play, as an ongoing rehearsal of reality, enables us to become familiar with playing in our small world within the World. There we can also acquire an accepted and familiar identity. For a long time this could be a comfortable choice. But nowadays it is quite hard to maintain a clear-cut "personality," capable of adapting to the innumerable changes going on all around us. Circumstances change, roles change, and each human being has to redefine her own identity, above all struggling for recognition in every scene she has to play.

Yet one can use one's innate inclination to play, not only to check reality but essentially to seek out a larger spectrum of alternatives. The aim, in that case, is to discover aspects of life capable of fitting and enhancing the authentic inner self. Experiencing play, we discern a sort of crossroads. Here we have to decide whether to continue chasing after the latest trendy role, position, or ephemeral and superficial identity or opt for being ourselves. In other words, we are invited to decide whether to remain a slave to this false self – shaped by external manipulations towards narcissist individualism – or to invest in our capacity to play. In the latter case, we discover elements of life to fit our uniqueness. Here we may create our individuality.

Leisure space is the arena where alternative issues, hidden by the routine game of life, can appear. Still this space may also become the oppressive atmosphere of a void. In this second result, it becomes the sphere of casual leisure, with the omnipresent temptations of consumption and the leisure industries. Still, as argued in the next chapter, leisure and consumption are not identical, thus the door is opened to the possibility of achieving individuality with little or no recourse to the leisure industry.

4

Leisure and Consumption

Consumption, says Russell Belk (2007, 737), "consists of activities potentially leading to and actually following from the acquisition of a good or service by those engaging in such activities." We are dealing here with monetary acquisition, defined in this book as either buying or renting with money a good or service. Bartering, borrowing, stealing, begging, and other forms of non-monetary acquisition are deliberately excluded from this definition and hence from these pages. Moreover, consumption through monetary acquisition is intentional. As such, receiving gifts falls beyond the purview of this work, because giving a gift springs from the intention of the giver rather than the receiver.

One reason for including the present chapter in this book on leisure and individuality is that there is in the literature on consumption a tendency to say little about leisure other than to relate it generally to such behaviour. For example, Daniel Cook (2006, 313) argues that "we don't live near or beside consumer society, but within it. Consequently we don't seek, experience, make or find leisure and recreation anywhere else." McDonald, Wearing, and Ponting (2007, 495) hold that leisure "has become an escape from the pressures of the competitive individualized labour market through the process of therapeutic consumption. The importance placed upon the acquisition and consumption of commodities has resulted in fetishism ... over-consumption, luxury fever." Consider the following UK statistics:

- Shopping is the top leisure activity and accounts for 37 per cent of all money spent in England.

- More than five million mobile phones are thrown away each year in the UK.
- The cost of an average handbag is £76, with the average woman in her thirties owning 21 and adding a new one every three months. This can escalate to expenditure of more than £9,000 on handbags over a lifetime.
- Some 50,000 Nintendo Wii consoles were sold in the first 12 hours after the gaming device went on sale in the UK.
- The average lifespan of an mp3 player is less than three years. The average 18- to 25-year-old changes their mobile phone every nine months, with the average over 25-year-old changing their handset every 14 months.
- The combined UK box-office returns for *Shrek the Third*, *Spider-Man 3* and *Harry Potter and the Order of the Phoenix* in their first weekends were £44,992,045.
(From "Spend, Spend, Spend: Where the Money Goes," by Ifunanya Ifeacho, included with an interview of political scientist Benjamin Barber [2009] by Sophie Morris)

In other words, it is common in scholarly circles to view leisure as little more than the purchase of a good or service.

Yet there is considerable evidence supporting the observation that leisure *cannot* be equated with consumption (for a review, see Stebbins 2009). In fact a number of leisure activities are essentially non-consumptive, for which the cost is nil or negligible. So leisure and consumption are by no means always an identity. One reason for this involved relationship between the two is that they are, in general, motivated substantially differently: the end of consumption is to *have* something, to possess it, whereas the end of leisure is to *do* something, to engage in an activity. Be that as it may there are times when consumption and leisure are so closely aligned as to make it impossible to distinguish the two, as seen in the examples of a collector chasing down a rare coin or a musician buying a fine old violin. The process of acquiring such items is seen by these two as very much a part of their serious leisure. Nevertheless, such situations are exceptions to the proposition just presented.

In other words, leisure and consumption are not always the same thing. Our goal in this chapter is to examine in detail the complex relationship between leisure, consumption, and individuation. The basic concept for our discussion is "buying individuated identity." This practice takes different forms depending on the mode of consumption, five of which will be examined subsequently.

BUYING INDIVIDUATED IDENTITY

When viewed as a quest for personal identification, much of modern consumption may be understood as falling into two great motivational classes. One is the search for social identity: some people want to show through buying a good or a service that they belong to a particular collectivity or have a particular status. For them this is a matter of establishing their social distinctiveness. That collectivity might be a group of friends, an organization, a community, a social movement, or what Maffesoli (1996) describes as a postmodern "tribe" (defined in chapter 2). The status sought might be that of rich person, fashionmonger, or fan of a professional sports team. The idea is to purchase a certain good or service that shows they are a member of this group or status category, many if not all, members of which have also made the same kind of purchase.

Examples of expressions of status category and collective identity are legion. The man who buys a Rolls Royce flaunts his status in the economic elite. The woman who owns a luxury condo sends a similar message, albeit by way of a different medium. People who pay to see an evening of boxing matches present themselves as members of a taste public quite different from that of people who buy tickets to see a Shakespearean play. And religious devotees who buy and wear a burka, turban, or yarmulka signal their allegiance to the corresponding faith and religious organization as well as, possibly, a related ethnic group (e.g., turban, Sikhism; local Sikh temple, Punjabi).

The other motivational class, and the one on which this book is centred, is the search for individuated identity. Here some people seek a good or service to enhance their individuality, as persons standing out from all collectivities having any relationship with the purchase. Their goal is to appear as a distinctive individual, like no one else the people in their circles have ever seen or known. Any purchased good or service tailor-made for a particular person could have this effect, for example, a special suit of clothes, a fine handcrafted violin, a unique parcel of land, or a personal chef hired to prepare exactly to taste all a person's meals. A man who owns so many ties that he appears to his associates to be wearing a different one each day is individuated in this way.

Nonetheless the practice of buying individuated identity is sometimes a matter of perspective and degree. Thus, those who go in for Shakespearean theatre have this distinction in common, but simultaneously stand out from all other collectivities and are thereby individuated at this social level. The same may be said for the owners of Rolls Royces and luxury condos. This situation is possible because the collectivities in question are relatively small but culturally important. By contrast hobbyists who spend money on, for example, equipment and material to make objects with metal constitute a very small proportion of the population which also engages in an activity having little cultural visibility. We may say, then, that consumer-related individuated identity may be either unique or social.

We acquire consumer-related individuated identity through at least five different modes of consumption: conspicuous consumption, adoption of commercial innovations, competitive compassion, shopping as leisure, and tourism. At this exploratory stage of the study of individuation, this list must be seen as not necessarily exhaustive; further thought and research could reveal still other modes.

Conspicuous Consumption

Thorstein Veblen, an American economist who wrote mostly between 1899 and 1923, is generally credited with having pioneered the idea of conspicuous consumption. In his celebrated work, *The Theory of the Leisure Class* (1899), he argued that leisure could be used to demonstrate status and power in modern industrial society, such that this practice resulted in a distinctive leisure class. Nevertheless use of wealth in this way is of relatively recent origin. Historically societies were unable to produce a level of material goods beyond that needed for subsistence. But eventually parts of some societies – the main examples being the industrial and post-industrial societies of today – came to enjoy a surplus of these goods, which raised questions about how the surplus is controlled, distributed, and used. "Control," "distribution," and "use" refer, in effect, to sets of options, one of which is conspicuous consumption. Here use is manifested in the purchase and hence ownership of distinctive goods and services available only to people who have the money (control) to buy them (distribution).

Veblen held that conspicuous consumption rests substantially on "invidious comparison." The basis for such comparison is ownership of distinctive consumer goods and services, or goods and services consensually recognized as indicators of their owner's accumulated wealth. This consensus was, in Veblen's day, shared by the wealthy elite, and it centred on having the taste to make the "right" acquisitions. In other words, it is sometimes possible to pay a great deal for an object or a service, but still fail to buy one regarded by this elite as demonstrating financial and cultural sophistication. Consider a modern example. Two wealthy people spend $10 million to have their mansions built, but one of them (the less sophisticated) has tastes for interior design that are judged by leisure-class standards as "plebeian," tastes that compare poorly with those of the other (more sophisticated) buyer.

Although Veblen did not address himself to the possibility, invidious comparison can also lead to individuation. That is, conspicuous consumption can sometimes become a vehicle for individuation. Continuing with the example just given, a wealthy owner could become individuated for his or her unique house, say, one architecturally designed and professionally decorated and landscaped to the specifications of that person. Such individuation could also be accomplished with a custom-built automobile. Patricia Kranz (2008) described how "one-upmanship" works these days among some contemporary billionaires. They clearly operate in a consumptive league of their own. One avenue some have chosen for conspicuous individuation, in addition to owning a private jet, a couple of mansions, and a Rolls-Royce or two, is having a magnificent and unique private motor yacht. According to Wikipedia ("List of Motor Yachts by Length," retrieved 27 November 2012) the longest – *Eclipse* – measures 533 feet. It belongs to Roman Abramovich of Germany. He one-upped Sheik Mohammed bin Rashid al-Maktoum in 2009, whose boat *Dubai*, built in 2006, had been the longest at 531 feet.

The examples in the preceding paragraph are, by the way, manifestations of project-based leisure. Owners must work closely over a specified period of time with an architect or boat-builder to get what they want in a distinctive mansion or yacht. Once it is completed the project comes to an end. We will return later in this chapter to individuation by way of project-based leisure.

In the meantime note that other instances of conspicuous consumption offer the buyer some casual leisure, though whether they produce individuality seems a more tenuous judgment. These include owning an expensive condo as second or third residence in a high-class resort, renting the penthouse suite in a swanky hotel, and holding season tickets for the most expensive loge available for watching the ballet. Finally, as an instance of conspicuous consumption of services in this century, note that, in England and particularly in Central London, use of butlers by the extremely wealthy as evidence of their elevated status is now said to be rivalling the extent of the practice in Victorian times (Binham 2008). Such lofty expenditures are available to a reasonably wide swathe of wealthy people, perhaps too wide to generate distinctiveness in their circles.

Still more down to earth we find numerous instances of modern, conspicuous, casual-leisure-related consumption in circles of people with varied but limited amounts of money for spending on personally individuating display. The electronic marketplace offers many an opportunity to look better than one's peers such as by purchasing the latest and most expensive iPod, video camera, or laptop computer. For a period of time Motorola's RAZR mobile phone was the rage among teenagers and young adults. It will be noted shortly that early adopters sometimes fall into this category, and that some later adopters may also shine this way if the item in question is sufficiently costly to dampen widespread sales. Here, too, individuation may be possible.

One well-known further explanation for such conspicuous consumption is Bourdieu's ideas about how people in power define such "aesthetic" ideas as "taste" (Bourdieu 1979, 41). His research showed how social class can determine the likes and interests of its members, and how taste- and class-based "distinctions" can become ingrained in daily life. In other words, the drive for individual distinctiveness, in part, reflects the person's class background. Not any old thing is consumed conspicuously; rather it must have merit in the eyes the consumer's reference group.

Adopting Commercial Innovations

Commercial innovation, more so today than ever, is a vast field strewn with new inventions of objects and processes. All areas considered – engineering, computing, aeronautics, automotive, medical, environmental, and others – the current rate of invention is staggeringly high. Still the sheer existence of something new does not inevitably lead to either quick or widespread adoption by targeted adopters. More precisely, with many inventions there are early adopters, later adopters, and non-adopters, or people who reject the newcomer (Rogers 2003).

Early adopters commonly pay a higher price for the new item or process than later adopters, primarily because, by the time the second enter the market, the pool of possible buyers is typically much larger. This reflects an economy of scale at the production level, wherein certain earlier start-up costs of the product, including those of its development, are offset by later sales at reduced prices to a substantially greater number of buyers (for an example of this pricing cycle for video games, see *Economist* 2008).

Thus, given the higher cost of the product at initial entry into the market and the prestige that often comes with owning or using the latest commercial innovation, the stage is set for a distinctive kind of modern-day conspicuous consumption and accompanying individuation. Early adopters may have to pay somewhat more for a recent invention, but this demonstrates financial capacity to do so and allows them to simultaneously

bask in the warm adulation of other buyers who also fancy owning it. On a much more ordinary level than the one-upmanship of
billionaires described earlier, such display is evident among early
adopters of the latest technological advances in cameras, mobile
phones, personal digital assistants, television screens, laptop
computers, computer software, and on and on, many of which
are used in leisure. Likewise an enthusiastic avant-garde emerges
around purchase of the latest innovations in tools, automobiles,
household appliances, and recreational equipment.

All these early adopters, to the extent conspicuous display
motivates them to buy the latest innovation in a certain consumer item, may also become authorities of sorts in their circles
of friends, relatives, and acquaintances who are interested in it.
Not only do early adopters enjoy the prestige of possessing an
unusual and conceivably valuable, useful good or service, they
also get contacted as sources of information about the good or
service. Added to the prestige of ownership of something unusual
but intriguing is the prestige of being an expert about it, itself a
kind of individuation.

In the typical case individuation by way of early adoption is
usually a short-lived, local status. Chances are that later adopters will soon arrive in much larger numbers, diluting, if not completely effacing, the distinctiveness of those few who were first to
buy. And, of course, by no means all the products and services that
lure a venturesome set of early adopters succeed in attracting a
decently large flock of later adopters. Moreover, with insufficient
numbers of the second, the first have no social mirror in which
to view their individuality, meaning that in effect they have none
in this area. We observed in chapter 2 that through individuation people become distinctive human beings. This status enables
them to enjoy a special personal identity within one or more of
the social circles in which they participate during their daily and
weekly rounds. In commercial innovation those circles consist of
would-be later adopters who, if they fail to show up in sufficient
numbers, because they dislike the product (e.g., the Edsel Ford
automobile in the late 1950s, the Segway electric scooter since
2001), then deprive the early adopters of the individuation they
could have otherwise enjoyed.

Competitive Compassion

According to the *Cambridge Learner's Dictionary* (2007, xviii) competitive compassion is expressed "when people give money to a charity (= an organization that helps people) because they want to seem kinder than other people. *It was competitive compassion which led people to give so much money following the floods*" (emphasis in original). The floods in question were those caused by the tsunami of late 2004 that devastated several countries in the Indian Ocean. Misty Harris (2008) maintains that such compassion is "a trend quickly turning philanthropy into an exercise in self-congratulation." Writing about Canadians she observed that some wealthy people are parading on Facebook their contributions to charity by, for example, talking about the money they have raised or the number of friends they have managed to rally to their favourite charity or non-profit organization. Harris says that, "Celebrity Apprentice and Oprah's Big Give have transformed philanthropy into a game show, with players competing as teams but being judged as individuals in the fight to be the ultimate altruist."

In short, here we have yet another mode of consumption capable of generating individuality. But the good being purchased is unique social esteem, which is, however, intangible compared with such tangible consumer goods as cars and tickets to a football match. Intangible but nevertheless real, in the Durkheimian sense of being a collective representation *sui generis*.

The preceding two paragraphs focused on the competitiveness of compassion as expressed by individuals. Nevertheless, this term, at least in the present-day popular media, is also applied with some frequency to the donations of national governments and, to a lesser extent, those of major private-sector organizations. Since this chapter does not treat conspicuous consumption by social units bigger than families, competitive compassion by larger groups will not be examined here. It is, however, a subject well worth exploring, albeit one that would take us too far afield from the topic of this volume.

Though not known by this label, competitive compassion did exist in Veblen's time. Instead he preferred to write about donors of bequests who had "other motives" in addition to the altruistic one of serving humanity:

> An example of this is seen in the administration of bequests made by public-spirited men for the single purpose (at least ostensibly) of furthering the facility of human life in some particular respect. The objects for which bequests of this class are most frequently made at present are schools, librar- ies, hospitals, and asylums for the infirm or unfortunate. The avowed purpose of the donor in these cases is the amelior- ation of human life in the particular respect which is named in the bequest; but it will be found an invariable rule that in the execution of the work not a little of other motives, fre- quently incompatible with the initial motive, is present and determines the particular disposition eventually made of a good share of the means which have been set apart by the bequest. (Veblen 1899, 226)

Veblen then elaborated on this observation with another: some buildings meant to serve these humanistic interests were instead constructed according to the "canons of conspicuous waste and predatory exploit." In other words, publicly visible parts of the structure were designed to impress with their pecuniary excel- lence rather than to enhance its effectiveness for those it was supposed to serve. Veblen placed this discussion under the rubric of the "survivals of the non-invidious interest," showing thereby how this humanitarian interest clashes with the selfish interest of conspicuous display. When it came to public visibility of the bequest, the latter commonly took precedence over the former.

As has been true of much of what has been said in this chap- ter about modern conspicuous consumption, the competitive compassion of today is far more general than the so-called non- invidious bequests of Veblen's time. The latter were gifts from the men of the non-working leisure class, whereas the former incorporates a much broader group of well-heeled men *and* women who have amassed significant sums, which they then give to charity. This is money gained from ongoing employment and investments bought with its fruits. Nor are the twenty-first-century competitively compassionate philanthropists, as a group, as wealthy as the leisure-class man of yore. Many of the first are, by today's standards, mere multimillionaires who give away comparatively small amounts of money, as measured across a period of nearly 120 years with inflation of national currency and what it can buy taken into account. And then, too, Veblen's leisure class never had the relatively inexpensive, diffusional advantages of the Internet and the popular television show to broadcast compassion as conspicuous display.

Shopping as Leisure

Shopping is what people do when they "shop," which is to go to a shop, store, or office to view or purchase a good or service, if not both. Broadly conceived of, today's shop is increasingly an online entity, even if the traditional shop seems destined to continue to play an important role in consumption. And people still contact shops at times, using the telephone and ordinary mail to discuss goods and services or make purchases. This is how many of us buy insurance policies, arrange for landline telephone service, reserve tickets to the opera, order a pizza for home delivery, and the like.

Shopping may be an obligatory or a leisure activity, a distinction that has been empirically validated in several studies. Prus and Dawson (1991) were the first to analyze the two types. Pasi Falk and Colin Campbell (1997) later covered the same ground, setting out the same twofold typology and underscoring for both types their impact on the self. The latter two also list in their bibliographic appendix a number of their earlier papers bearing on this same conceptualization. Most recently John Robinson and Steven Martin (2008) have analyzed thirty-four years of data collected by the General Social Survey in the United States in an effort to identity the activities in everyday life that make people happy and those that make them less so. Among their findings that bear on the topic of shopping as leisure and that clearly relate to consumption are those showing grocery shopping to be considerably less enjoyable than "other shopping" and eating meals away from home. The first would seem to be a disagreeable obligation, while the second two are leisure activities.

The spotlight in this section is on shopping as leisure, shopping that people like to do. Several observations may be made on this free-time activity. First, window-shopping is by far the best-known expression of such leisure. Here the shopper enters the marketplace for the enjoyment of seeing displays, looking at different creations and packaging of consumer items, fantasizing perhaps on how these might fit in that person's life, and so on, all without direct intention of buying the item of interest. This is casual leisure of the sensory stimulation type, in which curiosity plays a primary role (see figure 1, chapter 2). True, window-shoppers may buy something they have seen, perhaps because they have discovered a need for it, it has decorative value for home or office, or they have been looking for the item for some time and now, unexpectedly, have finally found it, even though they had not set out that day intending such.

Another type of shopping as leisure is that done in service of a serious leisure interest. Amateurs and hobbyists, in particular, must occasionally buy goods the purchase of which can be most pleasant. A horn player sets out to find a new and better horn, a coin collector goes shopping for missing parts of his collection, a kayaker patronizes her local dealer to buy a new, lighter, and more streamlined boat. The immediate outcome is the prospect, made possible by the purchase, of better and more fulfilling execution of the hobbyist or amateur passion. Furthermore, the process of purchase itself commonly proceeds from a background of considerable knowledge and experience relative to the best products and their strengths and weaknesses.

Such knowledge is central to the development of a positive sense of self, which Prus and Dawson argued can emerge from some kinds of shopping done for leisure. More to the point of this book, here is where shopping can serve to individualize a person. The horn player knows the best horn to buy, where to buy it, and that he will be distinguished among his musical associates as the owner of such a fine instrument. His individuality lies not in having merely bought a better horn, but in having bought the best, something very few other musicians can afford. This same scenario could unfold for the woman who buys a top-of-the-line kayak. Individuality for the stamp collector could rest on having the knowledge, money, and good luck, to be sure, to find a rare philatelic gem that few other collectors, if any, have found.

Of course there are times when serious leisure enthusiasts must also engage in some obligatory shopping of their own, such as making the occasional trip to the store that sells art supplies to buy paint or brushes or to the string instrument shop to arrange for repairs on a violin. The main purpose of such shopping is likely no more pleasant than certain routine purchases are for many people (e.g., buying petrol, using banking services, having prescriptions filled), though mercifully, it occurs much less often. Moreover, the tedium of such errands may be alleviated in part by doing some window-shopping while in the store. So the painter might browse the easels or the selection of frames. The violinist might look over the violins that are for sale or consider various musical accessories like metronomes or music stands.

Tourism and Individuality

Today shopping is a significant part of modern urban tourism the world over. As Bill Martin and Sandra Mason (1987, 96) have observed: "shopping is becoming more significant to tourism, both as an area of spending and as an incentive for traveling." Today no tourist guidebook of a world city would be without a section on shopping, typically running from high-end clothing and gadgetry shops to low-end flea markets and bargain stalls. Moreover, small communities, even villages, when sufficiently interesting in themselves and within the orbit of a larger tourist zone, tend to be bristling with tourist-oriented shops, several of them purveying local arts and crafts. And note how window-shopping is fostered by the ubiquitous gift and souvenir boutiques that are strategically situated to attract and tempt patrons as they exit today's museums. And then there are the flamboyant shopping sections of the big international airports. They combine the enticements of duty-free bargains with the tonic of window-shopping to passengers about to endure the tedium of a lengthy flight and those who have just escaped this state after disembarking one.

Tourism can present a variety of opportunities for conspicuous consumption, as manifested in a highly unusual destination, service, or purchase, if not a combination of these. In such circumstances individuality is a possible outcome. On occasion tourists buy something – often a souvenir – that individuates them among their friends and relatives. A person returning from India with a magnificent silk oriental carpet, the Arctic with a fine Inuit soapstone carving, or Africa with unusual native woodwork becomes distinguished by dint of these possessions. Alternatively the tourist might venture somewhere off the beaten path, as by taking a train trip across Siberia, a boat trip to Antarctica, or a cultural and wildlife safari through Tanzania. In so doing these tourists, to the extent that they have been where their associates have never been, individuate themselves through their travels.

Elite tourism offers opportunities for conspicuous project-based leisure and corresponding personal individuation. It is vividly exemplified in the new interest in space tourism. Wikipedia ("Tourism," retrieved 11 January 2008) says this "is a recent phenomenon of tourists paying for spaceflights, primarily for personal satisfaction." Space Adventures, which offers trips to the International Space Station, has individuated seven tourists between 2001 and 2009. As of 2012, space tourism opportunities are limited and expensive. Nevertheless, this "elite-elite" tourism has been predicted to come down in price in the next decade or so (McKinley 2012). More down to earth, so to speak, are the extravagant ocean cruises, where well-heeled guests may conspicuously consume by booking the most expensive state rooms on one of the most celebrated luxury liners. And, for $65,000 (includes a guide and a Sherpa or two) and a good amount of physical conditioning, anyone these days can complete the non-technical climb up Mt Everest's north side to gain the coveted title of World Class Mountaineer (Kodas 2008).

Is interest in touristic individuation related to age and age category? We know of no research on this question, but hints that there might be such a relationship do exist. For instance how many youthful backpackers tour as they do in search of individuating experiences? Thus, in Israel young people used to travel from six months to a year in exotic regions, often India or South

America. This started with few pioneers in the 1970s and became a must for all, a tacit obligation felt just after serving in the army and working in temporary jobs to earn money. Now, the practice is so widespread that a new trend has recently emerged among upper-middle-class young people: they skip this step in their adult socialization expressly to differentiate themselves from the "crowd." Johnson (2010) writes about the quests of some of the elderly for "never-ending adventure." He cites experts in the area who maintain that tens of millions of older men and women possess remarkable vitality, while pointing out that a vibrant leisure and tourism industry has sprung up to serve their interests. These participants want activities that are unusual for their age, if not for every age, among them long and arduous bicycle, hiking, and skiing trips.

CREATED WANTS

Now it is time we come to grips with a classic pair of concepts in economics that bear substantially on the contents of this chapter, notably *need* and *want*. We have been running comfortably along until now with loose usage of these two ideas, which in this chapter, however, demand more careful application. In traditional economics a need is seen as having a physiological or biological basis. As such it is essential for maintaining life, for instance, needs for food, air, water, shelter, clothing, and sleep and, let me add following Robert Wilensky (1978), essential for meeting an obligation. A want, by contrast, is significantly less essential to life; it is a desire or wish, which when fulfilled makes our existence more agreeable, possibly even more worthwhile.

The process of the commodification of leisure is germane here. Wearing and McDonald (2003, 60) define it as "the notion of purchased leisure governed by the market economy with the focus on profit. The leisure experience becomes a commodity to be bought, sold, and manipulated with this market fundamental in mind." In commodification, wants and needs are to be exploited to the advantage of the seller of a particular good or service. This is not to deny that buyers may be pleased with the good or service they have now been persuaded to want or need (and then buy), but as discussed below, critics of commodification point out that this process can also be both exploitative and detrimental to the social and economic situation of the exploited individual.

Moreover, there are times when need and want are not so easily separated. The obligatory, non-physiological/biological need is exemplified in such situations as: John needs to help Mary move because he promised this service; Mary needs to attend a meeting because she promised to chair it. But, in line with discussion in the section on serious leisure, these two instances of obligation might be seen by John and Mary as pleasant. In such cases they both need and want to fill the obligation.

Much of what has been said so far in this chapter has been concerned with wants and their fulfillment. Moreover, some wants start out as needs but, for some people, get transformed into desires, often by commercial interests. These desires when realized make life more agreeable. This transformation further shows how the line between the two concepts can be fuzzy, as Baudrillard observed in his statement on the ideological genesis of needs (1981, 63–8). Were he alive today he might, as evidence of his stance, point to the claims made about the goodness of bottled water versus that drawn from the (properly) treated municipal supply. To drink water is to fulfill a need, but to drink commercially bottled water hyped as superior in flavour to tap water is to fulfill a want, a desire for water that tastes better than what flows from local taps.[1]

Any discussion of leisure and consumption must of necessity be concerned primarily with wants rather than needs, unless of course, the needs are commercially transformed into wants. We need food, but it is leisure to meet this need at an upscale restaurant. Put otherwise some people want to meet this need in this way, though they do not have to do so simply to survive. Patronizing such a restaurant is a recognized leisure activity, albeit not one for all people. But it stretches the imagination to regard the transformed need of drinking bottled water as a leisure activity. Wearing a designer coat could be viewed in the same light, as non-leisure, even while a much cheaper coat might keep its owner just as warm. Or the handyman or woman of the house wants to buy a recently advertised, good-quality screwdriver with which to make obligatory repairs there, an activity not likely to be seen as leisure. In short, some needs are commercially transformed into wants that result in leisure, whereas other such transformations do not have this outcome.

So most of what concerns the field of leisure and consumption are directly created wants, desires that never were founded on one or more basic needs. A good deal of research, and no small amount of invective (e.g., Lefebvre 1991; Barber 2007), has focused on the tendency in the world of sales and manufacture to create these kinds of wants in potential buyers. At times this has been accomplished by sensitizing people through advertising and in-person sales pitches to wants they may not realize they have. There is no shortage of examples: listing the threats that call for a security service, the benefits to health of a certain herb, and the advantages of a particular savings account.

At other times, potential buyers know what they need, but commercial interests believe they still have to be pushed to buy a certain need-fulfilling good or service. We considered this process in the earlier section on adopting new innovation. What is to prevent a seller from arousing in early adopters of, for example, a new kind of computer software a need for individuation, in this case met by possessing an unusual and conceivably valuable, useful good? The seller might also work to enhance sales by pointing out that early adopters may be sought out as sources of information about the product, adding thereby to the prestige of ownership that of expert. In this scenario, the early adopters know of their need for individuation, a sentiment the shrewd seller exploits.

The question all this raises for this chapter on leisure and consumption is just how forceful or demanding are these created needs? Do they amount to obligations that must be met? In line with our definition of leisure: free-time activities, to be regarded as such, must not be coerced. On the one hand, meeting some created needs might well be defined by some buyers as obligatory – among them, containing threats to security and gaining benefits to health. Given this outlook these people, were they to buy the service or product, would seem to be engaging in obligatory consumption. On the other hand, many a potential early adopter, though possibly enamoured of the new-found identity of pioneering owner of a new, exciting innovation and expert on its use and properties, might not, however, see this as an obligation. Such an outlook would preserve the leisure basis for this sort of consumption, even though the purchase was motivated, in part, by either a created or a stimulated need for individuation.

SELFISHNESS AND CONSUMPTIVE INDIVIDUATION

We noted in chapter 2 that selfishness is one of at least four conditions capable of undermining individuation. To build now on that discussion, it is most appropriate in a chapter on individuation and consumption to observe that leisure activities can become for some participants some of the time more or less uncontrollable (Stebbins 2007, 17–18). More precisely their leisure is capable of inspiring them to engage in it beyond the time or the money (if not both) available for it. For example, there seems to be an almost universal desire to upgrade: to own a better set of golf clubs, buy a more powerful telescope, take more dance lessons perhaps from a renowned (and consequently more expensive) professional, play more and more string quartets (doing so by purchasing more and more music), and so forth.

These are serious leisure pursuits, but the same may be said for the casual and project-based interests. It is distinctive in certain circles to own the latest wrinkle in cell phone technology, automotive accessories, or wearing apparel, although the price paid for these marks of distinction is apt to be high. It is the same for some projects. Consider, for example, the elite and thus individuated set of "peak baggers" (people who climb to the summits of mountains) who have conquered the highest mountain on each of the world's continents, collectively known in mountaineering circles as the "seven summits." Though arduous – the climbers must be in good physical condition – these are not technical climbs requiring specialized equipment, as well as knowledge of and experience in how to use it. In 1985, American climber Dick Bass became the first mountaineer to climb this group (Bass, Wells, and Ridgeway 1986).

But, as noted in chapter 2, there may be significant others who also have claims on the money spent for these individuating pursuits. Such a situation can become a bone of contention, providing fertile ground for the accusation that the "big spender" is being selfish.

CONCLUSION

This chapter shows that individuation through consumption may be achieved without spending huge sums of money. More precisely, in circles where money is in short supply, an "extravagant expenditure" there, though trifling by the standards of wealthier people, may be enough to individuate the buyer. The goal is to stand out favourably in one's own circles, acquired through a distinctiveness shared with no one else or at most a few others. Yet it appears that most of the time consumption only aids the search for individuation in an activity, rather than being the main individuating force itself.

How long does consumption-based individuation last? The broadest answer is that it lasts until so many other people have bought the good or service leading to personal individuation that it is no longer viewed as a distinctive acquisition. More particularly it would seem that early adoption of a new technological or other kind of innovation is significantly shorter lived than buying a durable and enormously expensive item of property, such as a yacht or a mansion, or purchasing an unparalleled and enriching tourist experience such as climbing Everest or flying to the International Space Station. Experiences of this nature live for many years in the memory of the participant as well as in the memories of that person's associates. These latter examples have no adoption curve, as most innovations tend to have.

As for acts of competitive compassion, unless memorialized with a plaque or its equivalent, they also seem to offer only a comparatively brief place in the sun of individuation. By contrast acquisitions intended to advance a serious leisure activity and having an importance sufficient to individuate the participant, like finding the rare stamp or buying a fine old violin, should endure. Indeed that distinctiveness could well endure for as long as the acquisition remains with the owner and he or she continues in the pursuit.

This reasoning suggests that individuation springing from goods or services bought to initiate casual leisure activities have low staying power vis-à-vis their project-based and serious leisure counterparts. In initiatory consumption people quickly consume, in one way or another, what they purchase, what they have. In other words, they do what they intended with the purchased item either immediately or reasonably soon afterwards. There are plenty of examples: the child buys a candy bar then eats it, a woman buys a theatre ticket then watches a play, and a man places a bet at a roulette table then watches the wheel spin. But let us say that the gambler placed a million-dollar bet. Win or lose this act quickly becomes the talk of the casino world, and he is immediately individuated because of it. But soon, too, he and his bet fall into oblivion, swamped by a multitude of current events of far greater magnitude than anything casino gambling can ever match.

Perhaps momentary individuation is better than none at all. But, to the extent that people want enduring individuation from their leisure, this chapter suggests they search for it in their serious and project-based activities. This last point stresses the two faces of individuation: wanting to belong to some social group and striving to differentiate oneself within the group. That is, we sometimes try to individuate ourselves in the eyes of certain other people and sometimes we try to be an authentically different person in our own eyes. We might say, by analogy, that it's possible to perceive when we enter into a house, if it reflects the inner individuality of the tenant or some impersonal decoration, trendy or not.

Art, the subject of the next chapter, offers both these possibilities. Painters strive for an individual style, by which they can distinguish themselves from other painters. But a particular painter might also ask how, apart from my distinctive artistic style, am I different from other people, fellow painters included? Is it my personality? Is it my style of dress? Is it my coiffure? Is it how and where I live? Questions like these are important, as illustrated next in the world of art.

5

Art in the Leisure Era

Whether or not to be one's genuine self, that remains forever a challenging issue.

At one time, except for a few "banished" people, identities were pre-established for us and ready-to-wear. People's identities were determined even before their birth. The little world in which they began life was the readymade stage where they had to play, for better or worse, a role already written in accordance with the identity they would have to assume. Their life trajectories were already well-known, and nobody – including they, themselves – asked who they aspired to be. The issue was only whether they would accomplish their role well and improve their status in the corresponding casting. Only a few have ever tried to rebel against their pre-scripted roles, and they have paid a penalty for that rebellion. This unreflective way of thinking, leading to a "mechanical" and collective identity, would be quite "comfortable" for the great majority. For example, this would be true for anyone who lived with clear-cut answers to essential questions such as: Where have I come from? Where am I going? Who am I?

Historically, identity would become a personal issue only in the rare cases of someone's losing their hereditary place in society. In between eras – the era of unthinkingly belonging to a clear identity and the present era characterized by "chaos," with "all ways of life open to us" – we had, at least in Western countries, a kind of substitute in the professional or occupational domain. For many decades, a profession or occupation, as someone's main role throughout life, could provide a solid basis for a definite identity, with accessories such as social position, security, and stability. This base was large enough to include the whole family. One was identified not only as an "engineer" but also as an engineer's wife or child, and so on. Even retired people could continue to define themselves by their former occupations.

In the era of leisure, work tends to be reduced to its most basic significance, i.e., that of making a living. The position in the firm and the related social position have become precarious and in any case are no longer sufficient to cover the whole of one's identity, which, in turn, has become more complex and entails a greater awareness of multiple facets of life.

Nowadays identity is no longer "automatic." The issue of self-identity is open-ended, and almost everyone has to find their own way to an acceptable response to that issue. Are we prepared for this kind of challenge? How could we clarify the vague sense of ambiguity about our self-image versus our self-acceptance and all its implications for the concrete reality of life? Have we an acceptable response to the issue within the growing global village, which seems to offer innumerable glossy forms of self-identity, ready-to-wear with their trendy labels? Free will is no longer a virtual attribute in the global village, and there is no longer an easy *escape from freedom* (Fromm 1941). As we said in chapter 1, the crucial issue nowadays is how to face up to one's freedom, or in other words, how to face up to one's total personal responsibility.

This process of accepting one's freedom and responsibility becomes acute in the leisure space, where time is no longer a pre-established order of appointments and to-dos, where the individual is confronted with himself outside of a compulsory schedule of roles and obligations. He is free to do or not to do; free to be or not to be alone with himself, alone with his substantial liberty.

What a challenge!

What a dilemma!

The priests of the new religion of consumption are right there watching over us and planning products to respond to any worrisome, obscure needs. In our consumer civilization, one can buy almost anything, perhaps even a clean self-image, or at least a momentary sense of individuality. You may have seen the classic slogan, often used by advertising campaigns: "our product is not in everyone's hands, but those who have it are not everyone." If you remember that consumption is the most popular target for a leisure occupation, you could suppose that malls are not only spaces to escape from existential pressures but also ample stages for self-determination. During recent elections in many countries, especially in Europe, the issue of the "right to consume," that is, increased purchasing power, has been very prominent: sometimes we can be confused and see that struggle at the same level of legitimacy as all the others clamouring for recognition (Honneth 1996).

Should consumption be considered a form of self-expression? Perhaps we could argue that through consuming various goods, we do express our taste, our preferences, our style, or in a word: our art of living. And talking about art, what place does it have in our search for our true identity?

ART, CONSUMPTION, AND INDIVIDUALISM

In January 1963, the media of the Western world covered in colourful detail the glamorous voyage of the *Mona Lisa*, on the ocean liner *France*, to Washington, DC. It had been requested for exhibition at the National Gallery, as well as at the Metropolitan Museum in New York City. More than 1.5 million people came to admire and to enjoy this Michelangelo masterpiece (Martel 2006). What should we make of this event of mass consumption of art, sustained by media campaigns? Could we compare the kilometric queues waiting for a ticket to meet, during counted minutes, the *Mona Lisa* with the recent nocturnal wait of thousands expecting to be among the first buyers of the latest *Harry Potter* or the new MacBook?

Are we in the presence of a simple commercial trend in search of ever greater markets or an initiative to create a more democratic society? Could we compare the intensive campaigns of marketing for a new retrospective of Chagall's works, for instance, with the political activism of Diderot and d'Alembert, gathering universal knowledge for the sake of making it accessible to larger audiences? Martin Luther did the same 230 years earlier, when he translated the Bible into German, a subversive achievement aimed at taking away from the elites in the church the exclusive access to the sources!

These are the most famous of such initiatives, which have become more and more frequent over the years. Many scientists invest a lot of effort in presenting the essential parts of scientific discoveries and achievements in an accessible language far from their specialists' esoteric jargon. Thanks to these numerous initiatives we can say that, nowadays, the average patient knows much more about medicine than physicians did two centuries ago. A similar phenomenon has occurred in literature, where hundreds of millions have come to have access to Leo Tolstoy, Ernest Hemingway, Victor Hugo, and others, with the huge accessibility of the films based on their novels. Many of these millions, motivated by a film they had seen, read the book and perhaps other works of the same author. This process is often put down as "vulgarization," a pejorative term implying that the superior and complex works were simplified, even debased to the point where the author's intent was essentially lost. Is this appellation a crude reaction of elites, trying to protect their threatened social status (Bourdieu 1987)?[1] Taking our cue from Bourdieu (1987) – who maintained that concepts have to be accessible to ensure their development – let us consider the various processes of vulgarization as potentially leading to enrichment but also to impoverishment, depending on the personal attitude of the individual.

With the *Mona Lisa* now in the Louvre again – isolated in a protected space behind prominent barriers – we can see those small crowds trying so hard to have a look. You can guess that most of these people would be disappointed to see how small and quite "insignificant" this great item turns out to be, scheduled in bold letters in the guidebook for their organized tour. Nevertheless they will go through the souvenir shop (there is no other exit) and buy a print of the painting as a tangible proof of their consumption-visit to the Louvre.

Visiting museums has become a must in mass tourism programs. Is this an expression of the instrumentalism of art?

Kandinsky (1956), a century ago, already said: "People with these books [catalogues] in their hands go from wall to wall, turning over pages, reading the names. Then they go away, neither richer nor poorer than when they came, and are absorbed at once in their business, which has nothing to do with art" (14). Most of this consumption of art does not differ from any other kind of consumption, bringing the consumer a compulsive sensation of being, of being involved, of being someone. Paraphrasing Descartes we can say: I buy, therefore I am. And the more I am able to buy, the more I am.[2] This existence is mainly that of a reflected image of one's self.

While we are walking through the halls of an exhibition, listening to a concert, standing in the grandiose site of Masada in the Negev Desert, or watching *Nabucco*, are we aware that this is our leisure space, our free time, our second chance to be ourselves? Are we aware of the infinite opportunities available to us? Or, on the contrary, are we returning to well-worn patterns and seeing the leisure horizon as the same vicious circle (limited for the sake of social survival) that, for a few decades now, has included regular portions of casual leisure consumption? This is still the art appreciation of someone focused on what others may think of them: they have "to be in," to be up to date with all the art events everybody is talking about. Entering into the realm of leisure, we enter into it in a way we are used to, stimulated by external factors and with the basic motive of appearing to be successful in some way.

THE MIRACLE OF ART

It can happen as we are acquiring, step by step, a new state of mind introduced by casual leisure, that we become aware of the possibility of something else, something outside of consumer society. You may see signs of your inner desire for meaning, for something of greater depth. Kelly (1987, 207) noted the central link between leisure and the arts. This link, he said, allows for "the possibility of meditation or contemplation, the creation of ideas and states of consciousness. Leisure in this sense is a context for creation oriented toward possibilities for the future."

Indeed, leisure is the main birthplace of the self, of the realization of one's own nature pursued purely for its own sake, not least in the realm of art.

We uncover the magic secret of any new encounter, when we come to meet somebody/something initially for some specific purpose but discover the human dimension, both in our partner and in ourselves. We go through the superficial and instrumental *I-It* and introduce ourselves to the essential realm of *I-Thou* (Buber 1958). We may discover, then, that beyond personality (this limited and externally dependent image of oneself anchored in the common game of life), one's profound nature, one's individuality, has been waiting – sometimes for ages – to have its proper say.

Sometimes, in our responding to the authentic appeal within art, this miracle happens. We really meet Jean Valjean and with him our most sincere desire for justice. We sense the resonating *Kiss* by Rodin, the desperate accomplishment of Babette in *Babette's Feast* (by Karen Blixen), the blinding absurdity of human conflicts in Goya's *Third of May*, a breath of hope in hearing the "Ode to Joy" by Schiller in the Ninth Symphony of Beethoven, and so many other expressions of human misery, desire, and hope. In those privileged instants we are no longer consuming, we are entering into another human dimension, a realm of both essential and universal feeling, the realm of art where one renounces "one's own personality for a time, so as to remain *pure knowing subject*, clear vision of the world" (Schopenhauer 1909, 240). The threshold of this genuine leisure realm, thanks to an authentic encounter with art, can be the right space of a new initiation (Cohen-Gewerc and Spector 2001) towards individuality. You can leave the domain of appearances; you are no longer concerned about images. You look for your inner being.

Art and leisure, essentially entailing freedom, allow us to transcend the need to consume and enter the challenging field of creation, a field of opportunities, of learning and discovering what creation can be: painting, music, drama are a few examples of the enticing prospect of "free-choice learning" (Packer 2006). You can meet these two areas of opportunity, leisure and art, at the crossroads of personal freedom, and there discover art, a realm beyond, which penetrates the no man's land between individualism's impulsive drive and the desire for individuality.

ART AS EXPERIENCE

Let us come back to the crowds of people who came to visit our famous *Mona Lisa*. Among all those visitors, we might suppose that a few individuals where truly touched. They did not leave the museum as they had entered it (Kandinsky 1956). They encountered some specific work or works which affected them, even if everyone differently. In the crowded circumstances of the gallery, you may suppose that, in a few cases, individual experience was unique and essential. In this sense, the leisure state of mind is a privileged place where, as in an experience of love, two experience each other as one, together throughout the whole world. Although the spectator's experience of art is less tremendous, it is no less crucial (Dufrenne 1967, 3).

Being at leisure means we are on vacation from customary commitments allowing our social survival, on vacation from our labelled image. We are free to pay full attention to our senses, despite their having their own limits. Aristotle stressed their limitations and also their central importance: "Further, we do not consider any of the senses to be wisdom. They are indeed our chief sources of knowledge about particulars, but they do not tell us the reason for anything, as for example why fire is hot, but only that it *is* hot" (Aristotle [1933] 1989, *Metaphysics*, 981b).[3] Among our senses, the most rich and complex is eyesight, which brings us innumerable data. And if that is the issue, we wonder: Seeing for what? Are we looking in order to identify something or with the aim of discovery?

This is where the tension lies between the established life game and the new paradigm for the leisure era. The first tends to instill in our awareness a common world view establishing a plan for our existence and its concrete doings, even if they appear to be changing in accordance with local or global trends. The aim of individual efforts is then to identify and mostly duplicate common patterns. The new paradigm looks forward and beyond; its motivation is not to reproduce but to create.

From this point of view, Paul Cézanne went beyond and consumed his whole life in trying to capture, through his limited human sight, the essence of Sainte Victoire, the mountain in front of his window. Looking for that essence Cezanne observed and described his mountain again and again and perhaps, in doing so, became the "clear eye of the whole universe" focused on that small part of it. Perhaps we could accompany Cézanne's pulse, when entering each morning into our small garden and gazing at it as if it were our first encounter, distinguishing that unique luminosity, that new shining leaf, that delicate emotion in ourselves, experiencing something of the universal harmony.

The leisure state of mind offers the opportunity to experience, at least in part, this process well-known to artists. It entails the tacit will to grasp the significance of passing events so that every instant in life becomes unique – an instant in which one may discover a further aspect of things, a fresh nuance. You can then use the whole range of your faculties, your capacity to sense, imagine, and understand new aspects that you generally ignored while involved in an efficiency-oriented, instrumental way of life. What a new perspective: to simply exist, to be, and to do, only for the sake of being and doing.

Art, let us remember, is useless by its nature. Yet it brings back to us the legitimacy of our essential affinity with existence, and our entire personal responsibility for our distinctions, metaphors, and the particular creation crystallized in the composition of our lives, as the ensemble of our choices. In leisure space, as in the realm of art, the models and patterns are only suggestions and every one may decide in any instance, which word, which sound, which brush stroke to add to the picture of one's life. Art experience, inspired by the serious leisure state of mind, means abandoning the idea of certainty, taking risks while entering into unknown locations, including our inner self. Leisure: moving forward in this territory, away from modular, self-certain patterns as our basic support, demands an alternative source of assurance.

To respond to the deep impulse to discover and create requires having inwardly the force to endure failure, alone. To renounce the conventional clearly demands effort – an effort that essentially implies courage.

Here, in this realm, doubly obliged to personal freedom as leisure and art, we are not looking for a scripted scenario, some small "world" inside the World. We are engaged in meeting the entirety of life. We have left the frenzied rush of superficial individualism, and we enter carefully into our still unknown individuality. Here, far from the illusory commonplace and familiar trends, we are invited to meet our entire self, to listen to all the nuances of our vitally legitimate senses and feelings. Thanks to art, we experience this extraordinary domain of life where a genuine expression of essential particularity can reach the most telling universality. At this juncture we can sense totally our vital being through our free aspiration to realize fully our part in the play of humanity.

Federico Garcia Lorca said that an artist is necessarily an anarchist, because it's hard to agree with the regime – any regime – working by every means at its disposal to "normalize" its citizens. Yet, for Garcia Lorca, being an anarchist doesn't mean being alienated. Freedom of artistic vision and freedom of thought, the common intrinsic requisites of art and leisure, enable the poet to receive and seize life's tempo as expressed by the poet's contemporaries, in its culmination or its distress; and through their particular existence, the poet can feel and express a little of the eternal human essence. Here lies the difference between narrow identity and uniqueness. Clear-cut identity tends to draw borderlines in order to separate; uniqueness looks forward for linkage.

From this point of view, no Spanish author could express better than Garcia Lorca the unique reality of his compatriots; yet there is no place on earth where someone is not moved by Yerma's cry, this woman humiliated by her sterility, and no language that does not announce the tragedy of the matador "at five o'clock, in the afternoon," this scream coming from the Spanish bull arena.

Let us also consider, in this respect, Giacometti. In what particular environment can we place his sculptures midway between existence and nothingness, but intensely seeking the absolute (Sartre 1984, 54)? Thanks to the immense horizons within leisure space, we can open our minds and declare, with Giacometti, how crucial it is to train our perceptiveness, being conscious that although we look from our essential, particular, and relative point of view, we do it with the genuine and deep aspiration to seize the whole thing, that is, its essence.[4]

In this sense, Giacometti is like Beethoven, Villa-Lobos, Picasso, Twain, Byron, Saramago, and so many others. We are of course aware of the immense gap between this similarity and the similarity obtained through "normalization." The first similarity comes out from the deepest uniqueness of individuals open to human affinity; the second is only an outer envelope asking for uniformity, an easy escape from the need to explore.

Being in the space of serious leisure, entering into the realm of art as actor and spectator, we may learn about ourselves and our humanity. An artist tends to consider every instant of his life as a challenge to his wisdom, which tries to decipher the abundance of signs his senses seize and gather. The art of life entails a multitude of nuances inviting the individual to find and choose his personal composition. Leisure time, let us remember, is a space beside the demanding arena of the life game, a space where we can do and experiment with things, and also without clear-cut "utility." A piece of art is as well, by its nature, something without utility for survival. Yet we are concerned with more than survival: we sense the inner demand for the significance, the meaning, that art can design in its own kind of language. Art language does not fix patterns; it only tries to draw the changing contours of life's vitality.

Leisure allows us to penetrate into the domain of art, not merely to pass through it. During our frequent stays in the realm of art, we can and we should discover and acquire this particular language, which will be a fine "souvenir" we can bring back with us to our conventional realm of life.

And what a souvenir!

Language is this great human resource which allows us to use words, notes, colours, shapes, etc., as the concrete expressions of our thoughts. An artist and a scholar can suggest in their minds, and in those of their listeners, the tangible image of raging waves, even thousands of miles from the sea. With the language of art we can express our wandering and unending search for the innumerable facets of life's essence. All the numberless poems about love cannot and will never prevent new poets from writing their own, personal, unique vision of this universal human emotion.

The free space of leisure is to the scenes of daily life (where being on stage means defined roles and their scripted lines) what art is to craft. The craftsperson has to reproduce an existing model; the artist aspires to create. The craftsperson multiplies existing objects; the artist adds new vital forms. To provide for the demand tourists, the craft industry has to make thousands of small copies of Michelangelo's *David*. The artist standing face to face with the block of marble had to extricate the sculpture, the unique one he already envisioned in his mind. As for our craftsperson, he works to transform raw materials into a known and established shape. An artist, with his personal idea, has to dialogue with the block of marble, which expresses its long history through its strata, texture, colours, and consistency. Thanks to this dialogue, the artist can go ahead, step by step, and extract the unique sculpture, which had been there waiting for him in this specific block, for ages.

In this crucial encounter, the marble expresses itself through its specific attributes and the artist succeeds in discerning the hidden sculpture waiting inside, and chisels away all the superfluous material. Although in this ideal description in art, as also happens in real life, nothing is totally necessary, the artist's freedom was a decisive ingredient and he knew that in this specific block were waiting various other latent sculptures. This sculpture was not the only one in the block of marble. This creation was born in the artist's mind waiting there until the happy meeting with the right piece of marble able to give birth to this unique sculpture, which would live its own life among the generations. As in other kinds of life, every couple gives birth to its own type of offspring, different artists would create other sculptures as fruitful dialogues with the same block of marble.

The secret of renewed life lies within the innumerable opportunities offered by ongoing time at the crossroads of necessity and hazard, with the significant addition of the inherent human free will. This essential aspect tends to dim at that level of existence where roles and commitments seem so obvious, although it is a comfortable realm in many aspects. However, it is a world that has tended to reduce, more and more, the significance of compulsory social roles. It is a growing contemporary phenomenon in that people are used to seeing rapid changes in all domains, the seemingly obvious is not quite obvious at all, and individuals find themselves disarmed at so many crucial turning points.

Remember that, in the old life game, a long-standing combination of social habits and obedient individuals left the "device" of freedom quite commonly unused. Nowadays, we can argue that every ten-year-old boy or girl experiences more freedom and makes more decisions than people a century earlier did, during their whole lifetime. Yet we must stress, again, that if people are more pressed to decide for themselves, it doesn't mean that they are really capable of doing so. Serious leisure and art can offer a rewarding new perspective in accomplishing this.

Thanks to leisure we can experience the refreshing sensation of that new initiation to life. Like a child who takes her first footsteps, we have to sharpen our sight and concentrate our attention. Thanks to art, one gains a renewed capacity for wonder, not so much as a superficial consumer but as one who has been initiated. Initiated into art, we refresh our curiosity for what is unique and appeals to the universal while we may go out of the marked paths in order to enlarge, consciously, the radius of our search for our humanity.

The self-evident has expired and we are quite ready for a new play in the open-ended theatre of life, even where we fail. We know that in coming to the new and the unexplored, we face the possibility of failing.[5] Entering into the realm of art, encouraged by our leisure state of mind, we are not merely escaping from conventional roles, looking for casual fun – we're not desirous of the new for the sake of being new, but for its potentiality to *renew*. We're not excited by some innovative look, but by the hope of a renewed vision.

For example, in the well-known painting *Lacemaker* by Vermeer, we observe a routine, banal scene as people of Vermeer's time would see it, and we wonder if anyone ever really paid any attention to it. Yet for more than three centuries, Vermeer has invited us to contemplate this unique appearance with a fresh look (and not simply with a vague sense of déjà vu) and have a chance to discern, beyond the instrumental narrative, a glimpse of spirituality accompanying the human presence. The lacemaker is wholly present in Vermeer's painting by that name; her intensely concentrated look testifies to her total dedication, and from this supposedly routine activity emanates a little of human existence. More than that, a connection arises between this anonymous lacemaker and the spectator: slowly her specific clothing and the Dutch surroundings give place to the universal and the human. A banal and fleeting anecdote breaks all the boundaries of time, space, ethnicity, all the boundaries that humanity has tried to build with the purpose of separating each individual from every other and from each one's own potential wholeness.

Again, in the film by Henri Verneuil, *The Cow and the Prisoner* (1959), we see the French prisoner (the actor Fernandel) trying to comfort a couple of worried German parents, telling them that if their son (a German soldier) is in Marseille – his city of birth – they can be assured! The sincerity in his appearance and in his words, together with the typical parents' worry, enable us to skip over their differences, over the event (a French prisoner escaping from Germany during the Second World War), over the circumstances (the dreadful war), and to rescue in each of the characters an authentic human being. By the magic of art we can meet within this very prisoner, in this very anecdote, the essence of his humanity and of ours. We can, of course, watch this film and laugh at the absurd situation and above all pass, burn, waste ninety minutes of our empty time; but we also have the opportunity to raise our view and enrich our awareness.

Leisure is free time – a free time, however, open to our whole being, our potential individuality. Leisure can be this valuable opportunity, provided that we have been initiated into it. Nothing can bring us into it better than art. Art doesn't see time as a multiplication of present moments but as a dimension of opportunities to look, and to renew a vision. The renewed experience of time in the realm of leisure, enriched by the language of art, invites us to a different encounter with it. It will no longer be a demeaning process, but a source of renewal and empowerment. Bergson said that "time is invention or nothing" (1983, 341). Time becomes, then, a basic resource in which we can be the artist of our personal existence as a noble part of the human adventure.

Taking up a new relationship with time leads us to free our minds from all kinds of divisions and consider our time, i.e., life as a whole. We unify our vision of life as a continuous becoming, conscious of our being while we are living. This wisdom acquired in the leisure field, thanks to our experience of art, now goes beyond the leisure moment and becomes relevant to life wherever we are and whatever we are doing. We have learned to be present, present with all our mental faculties, with all our senses and with the essential feeling of being totally there. Experiencing this sensation we discover the substantial presence of time beside us; time becomes our great friend.[6]

As great friends of time, we will pay attention to it, to all the aspects it entails. Returning to what we perceived as the instrumental, alienated game of life, we may discover – inspired by our fertile stay in the realm of art during our leisure time – that every instant of our existence contains more, much more in comparison with what we used to see in the obligatory rush of everyday life.

Being doubly free in leisure and in the realm of art, we sense the great responsibility of being human, that is, of being ourselves. Like Vermeer when he painted the commonplace gestures of a milkmaid, a woman reading, or a lady writing a letter, we will look at every instant of life as unique, and sense the numberless pulses of vitality within us and around us. From leisure, we take our freedom and our receptiveness. Freedom means that we are off the stage entirely and left without a scripted role: we can decide what to do in this "empty" time, and even do nothing. Becoming receptive means we have room in our minds to seize, to discern, and to receive not only what occurs outside but also and mainly what happens inside.

From art, in turn, we learn how to experiment with the entire use of our senses and our thoughts. Being free and receptive, assisted by your senses and reason collaborating in harmony, you are conscious of your individuality, your uniqueness, and at the same time of being an autonomous part of humanity. You can sense that you are absolutely present in every instant of life as your personal identity evolves in its continuity. You can then experience the increasing coherence of an inward form of individuality, which now exists beyond the image in the eyes of others. You are no longer led by an alienated egocentrism manipulated by an individualist and consumerist culture.

As an example, a few years ago, a young engineer told me that he would never marry or have children, because he wanted to have the use of all his money to buy tickets to all the concerts he liked, and to buy all the compact discs of the marvellous music he loved and enjoyed, and all this for himself. In his case, art seemed to have become his closed shelter and he perhaps didn't know that, while shelters may seem to be needed for a while, the fascinating, enriching, and challenging life is outside, in the open, in the inhabited, shared world. Individuality would means, on the contrary, a desire to sense our being, to meet, to discover, and to know, not only the surface and the wrap, but the essence – our essence.

CONCLUSION

Whether to be one's self and free is no longer a refined issue of the few. We are no longer a "depot" of quite ready, spare parts destined for the maintenance of autarkic communities. Life is no longer lived in public trains with class hierarchies and one unique driver. We are in the era of the private car in which everyone holds the steering wheel and has to choose a way of life at every crossroads, especially in the open spaces free of social obligations as in the growing areas of leisure.

Yet to be individual is now a recognized premise of our existence; and to suitably develop this premise, a personal challenge. Abandoned to ourselves, we may get lost within the multitude of situations, reactions, emotions, and thoughts – thoughts to which we tend to belong, more than they to us. How can we resist this all-conquering, disorienting individualism (Touraine 2005) based on the dictatorship of short-term desire (Lipovetsky and Serroy 2008).

The process of hyper-individualization and what Lipovetsky and Serroy call "Market Culture" (a recent evolution of the market economy) tends to disrupt, on a large scale, the consciences of individuals, their ways of life, their existences themselves. "The hypermodern world is disoriented, insecure, destabilized, not only casually but in daily life, in a structured and chronic way" (2008, 19) – welcome then to distraction!

"While the feeling of void is growing up," they continue, "more and more exciting ways appear to escape the darkness of a night without values, an abysm without aim and signification" (33). As we have said before, life offers more and more diversity, options, choices, opportunities, possibilities, and freedoms, but most of us are not truly prepared for a fruitful dialogue with them. There comes the pivotal role of leisure education (Cohen-Gewerc and Stebbins 2007) in which initiation into art can be essential to our self-knowledge. Schiller ([1794] 1909–14, letter 2) told us more than two centuries ago, that "the road of aesthetics must be pursued, because it is through beauty that we arrive at freedom."

Let us recall that free time, that is, leisure time as seriously pursued, can be a second chance to realize part if not all of the hopes and desires that did not fit with our commonplace social demands: professional, familial, and so forth. This can also be a moving re-encounter with our essential and neglected selves. The human desire of transcendence, with its treasures of sensitivity, is still there. It is lying somewhere in the depths, far from our incipient awareness, waiting for some singular crossroads at which we can be blessed by a momentous encounter with ourselves – which can be a way of becoming, in Touraine's expression, "a subject," "one who ... goes up to himself, what gives meaning to his life, creates his freedom and his hope" (2005, 189).

When someone experiences art as a complement to the leisure state of mind, he comprehends the amazing discovery that he exists, that he can be present in life, beyond any title, any function, any efficient role. He is totally present in life, independently of and beyond any task, and truly senses his freedom. Entering into art, as spectator or as a creator, is again "leaving one's own interests, wishes, and aims entirely out of sight, thus ... entirely renouncing one's own personality for a time, so as to remain *pure knowing subject*, clear vision of the world" (Schopenhauer 1909, 240). Through art we can experience the magic harmony of our essential and separate uniqueness and our being fully part of the whole universe.

Experiencing the mood of creation either as spectator or creator is like entering into some inner "apartment" where I take off the jacket, the tie, and the shoes, along with the outer envelope of a social role, and in this frame of mind sense the vital resonating of my whole being. I am there, in the workshop of life, close to the raw materials of the arts – notes, words, colours, and so on – in a crucial dialogue, trying with all my might to find the appropriate form to express part of my aspiration, the essence of my discernment, my perception, my insight into my life or rather, human life. Why couldn't we renew our vital energy for sensing and feeling our lives, and through this energy life itself, in the oasis of art where we could nourish and strengthen our uniqueness, that is, our individuality and its innumerable folds (Deleuze 1993), with the universal sources of deep desire?

Art in its pure form, free of any kind of utility or "interest," is a miraculous retreat, where our individuality can absorb vital resources in between bouts of the continual struggle for life, a "struggle" not only in terms of survival but in terms of significance. Leisure space, as the meeting point with one's self, can, despite the hegemony of consumption,[7] be an oasis of peace, where art constitutes the basic catalyst of one's emerging individuality. Art and serious leisure are powerful responses to the vanity and superficiality of contemporary life, while opening an authentic path leading from oneself to the world, from essential feeling to universal significance.

Let us remember that, in spite of being a personal and essential process, sincere self-discovery through serious leisure and art is our deep commitment to our community and to humanity as a whole. To be more allows us to be able to offer more. A responsible mother and father take care of themselves so they can take responsible care of their children. Could we not expect that, within the chaos of today's society, new kinds of communities would be germinating, communities as free associations of individuals engaged in the personal processes of self-searching (Cohen-Gewerc 2008)? Could we not hope that globalization would likewise lead us to mutually inspire rather than externally and intrusively standardizing one another? Do we not have enough faith in the human spirit to allow citizenship to transcend the two extreme poles: those of being either a passive instrument or an exigent consumer of the state? Could there be no contribution of serious leisure and creative art – with the consciousness it entails – to a new concept of solidarity, aspiring to enhance not only groups and narrow interests but essentially our common human destiny?

6

Community, Citizenship, and Globalization

In this chapter we place individuality in the larger social contexts of community, citizenship, and globalization as these three are advanced through leisure activities. It is important to show in detail that individuation is not only a personal matter: it can also have salutary consequences for society, sometimes on a world scale. Yet, as we have argued before in this book, individuation is not always positive. On the contextual level, as well, it can have deleterious effects. Let us start with the context of community.

COMMUNITY

In this section we consider, first, the relationship of individuality and alienation and, then, the relationship of individuality and participation. When does being distinctive isolate the individual in his community and when does this serve to deepen his attachments there? When does individuated leisure bring the individual into contact with other people in the community, beyond family, as experienced through outstanding, individuating performance in amateur, hobbyist, and volunteer activities? When do these performances become alienating, as manifested in selfish, exploitative, dishonest, immoral, conceited actions?

The two key concepts in this section are alienation and its opposite: participation. Melvin Seeman identified six kinds of alienation that have been studied over the years, of which two can spring from weak or wholly absent communal participation, the bitter fruit of an overpersistent search for individuality:

- *Cultural estrangement*, or individual rejection of commonly held values in the society versus commitment to existing group standards.
- *Social isolation*, or the sense of exclusion or rejection versus acceptance. (1972)

By contrast, *participation* is taking part or engaging in voluntary action, usually with others for their benefit as well as the benefit of the participant (Smith, Stebbins, and Dover 2006, 169). Since it is voluntary such participation occurs primarily in leisure. Here it proceeds along the lines of certain shared values, a condition we will examine in greater detail in our discussion of citizenship.

Alienation

When individuation is a major goal in the pursuit of serious leisure, alienation is a possible outcome. Below we look at five alienating ways of pursuing serious leisure to the point of becoming individuated: selfishness, exploitation, misrepresentation, immorality, and conceit.

SELFISHNESS   Selfishness was discussed in chapter 2 in the section on undermining the quest for individuality. What remains to be considered is the effect of selfishness on those who, despite their exploitation of certain others, manage to individuate themselves. How is it that such acts can then become alienating for the person thus individuated?

It has been argued elsewhere (Stebbins 2007, 75) that selfishness is part of the culture of leisure, a proposition based on Stebbins' observations over the years that many participants in all three forms share a tendency to act in this way. Moreover, this tendency and the problems it can spawn appear to be fully recognized in leisure circles, though admittedly, the matter has yet to be systematically studied. Selfishness roots, to some extent, in the uncontrollability of leisure activities. They engender in participants the desire to engage in them beyond the time or the money (if not both) available for free-time interests. As we said earlier, leisure enthusiasts are often eager to spend more time at, and money on, the core activity than is likely to be countenanced by certain important others who also make demands on that time and money.

Additionally enthusiasts (some would say "addicts"; Stebbins 2010b) in extreme sports and hobbies may be accused of being selfish by intimates who will suffer mightily with what the latter see as the probable death or serious injury of the former. In these examples the intimates may conclude, sooner or later, that the enthusiast is far more enamoured of the core leisure activity than of, say, the partner or spouse. When a participant, seemingly out of control, takes on too much of the activity or too much risk in doing it, imputations of selfishness from certain important others (whether overtly made or covertly held) are surely just around the corner.

Individuated performance in this kind of serious leisure is heady stuff, though mainly for the participant. It is easy to see how in searching for distinctiveness this person might resort to some selfish acts. Still, at least in volunteering, individuated involvement raises some prickly questions. Do its lofty ends – for example, providing the community in remarkable ways with amateur theatre, volunteering for an extraordinary number of hours for the Salvation Army, or providing the same lengthy service for the Olympic Games – justify the selfish means by which they are sometimes reached? Do the ends justify selfishness or other contentious practices along the way? When questions of this kind haunt individuated participants, the possibility of becoming alienated – of being socially isolated – takes root.

EXPLOITATION   Selfishness is exploitative activity, but does not in itself exhaust all opportunities for taking advantage of others against their will. People driven by a desire to stand out from the crowd by way of their leisure have other ways than self-ishness to exploit the community, which is in general to exploit small groups, large formal organizations, or local customs, or a combination of these. The alienation experienced in these circumstances is that of social isolation or cultural estrangement, sometimes both.

In exploiting an informal group the self-seeker takes unsanctioned advantage of all or a substantial proportion of the collectivity. For example, an amateur basketball player bent on individuating himself on the court could refuse to pass the ball to players in better positions than he to shoot at the basket. Instead this man too often attempts to score from his less advantageous place in the game at the moment. A woman singing in a community chorus, blessed as she is with a strong and well-trained voice, wants to distinguish herself by standing out vocally over the other singers in her section. The audience can hear her well, but at the expense of the balance of all voices, a quality that is the hallmark of good choral singing.

Instances of exploitation of large-scale organizations are legion, even if some of them are not about augmenting personal standing using this approach (e.g., organizations sometimes try to exploit each other). But individual distinctiveness is (possibly) enhanced when, for example, a member works hard to become organizational president by exploiting his present position there to reach this goal. To this end, he arranges – within his rightful powers – for collective events, say, seminars, parties, or workshops, at which he will strut his expertise. Or consider the woman who, as member of the organization's board of directors, strives for approval of a policy permitting her to hang some of her paintings in the office's reception area where numerous clients come and go. Assuming the policy is given the nod, this Sunday painter will gain exposure for her works and a modicum of progress toward individuation in this activity. In these examples we are speaking of leisure, of non-profit organizations and the volunteers who serve them.

How might people in search of distinctiveness become alienated when they exploit culture to reach their special status? Consider the norm of *noblesse oblige*, which is commonly translated from the French as "privilege entails responsibility." Let us say that the man in the preceding paragraph does become president of his organization, a position he now enjoys for its distinctiveness but at which he also fails to fulfill adequately his duties. For he is now exploiting the privilege of his presidency by devoting time to other interests that further individuate him, time that should be given to those duties. (We may say that he is also exploiting his organization.) As another example, note the people who seek distinctiveness by claiming to have had a religious vision, thereby rejecting scientific principles about the impossibility of such happenings.

MISREPRESENTATION Misrepresentation can be a route to alienation of the cultural estrangement variety. How many wealthy folk cheat on their income tax so as to retain more of their wealth? Some of these people then misrepresent themselves as richer than they really are, demonstrating their overt wealth and its distinctiveness to others in their circles by means of conspicuous consumption and display of enviable goods and services (Veblen 1899). Then there were those entertainment celebrities of the 1930s and 1940s who dishonestly used photography to distinguish themselves from others in their circles. Hannah Duguid (2008) describes this practice:

> It's the stuff of fantasy: a photograph of Joan Crawford with liquid eyes and flawless skin, her strong bone structure casting sculptural shadows across her face. There is no context, no setting: it is simply a close-up of her perfectly beautiful face. Crawford's troubled character is not apparent in these photographs, nor is her battle with alcohol; the ravages of life are painted over with clever lighting and a thick concealer.
>
> The photograph was taken by George Hurrell, head of portrait photography at MGM Studios in 1930. In those days, Hollywood studios employed full-time photographers who were responsible for creating a star's image. Those were the days of high glamour, when young women became sophisticated princesses, their allure heightened by their unattainability ... He spent hours with his subjects, perfecting their look. Their public persona was a creation, a brand, an image on to which people could project their fantasies and desires. They were not meant to reflect reality, or reveal anything about the women's real character – it was all made up.

As still another example of using misrepresentation to bolster individuality, consider the use of performance-enhancing drugs. Some use of these substances is, to be sure, intended simply to make the athlete a decent competitor, not one who stands out above the crowd. Yet a few do hope for individuality by these means. Thus, baseball professional Mark McGwire held the all-time major league baseball home-run record (achieved in 1998) until Barry Bonds outdid him in 2001. Wikipedia ("Mark McGwire," retrieved 11 March 2010), citing the Entertainment and Sports Programming Network (ESPN) maintains that in 2010 McGwire admitted taking steroids, illegal in professional baseball since 2006. Bonds is presently suspected of the same impropriety. To the extent that these allegations are true, both men might be seen as trying to project a public image as power hitters, a personal quality we expect to be developed through a combination of inherited ability and rigorous training, rather than through chemical enhancement. These are all instances of individuated occupational devotees, described in chapter 2 under the heading of occupational devotion.

IMMORALITY It could be argued that misrepresentation is immoral. If so the level of immorality is low compared with the delicts covered in the present section. Here we examine deviant behaviour, human acts in violation of certain moral norms in the community. Casual or serious, deviant leisure mostly fits the description of "tolerable deviance." Although its contravention of certain moral norms of a society is held by most of its members to be mildly threatening in most social situations, this form of deviance nevertheless fails to generate any significant or effective communal attempts to control it (Stebbins 1996b, 3–4).

The main examples of immorality leading to individuality in leisure seem to be found in deviant serious leisure, in deviant science, politics, and religion (Stebbins 1996b, chap. 10). Still the large majority individuated deviant scientists and religionists are making a living from their activity, with famous hobbyists (famous for that reason alone) being therefore unusual. It appears that deviance of these two varieties has a following willing to pay for a service, whether as casual entertainment or as serious consultation. So it is that most experts in ufology, water-witching, clairvoyance, telepathy, astrology, and the like – all deviant sciences – can make a living at their trade and even become well-known there. Moreover it is possible that some could be shown to be occupational devotees. The same may be said for certain religious leaders, among them, Sun Myung Moon of the Unification Church (Moonies), David Koresh of the Branch Davidians, and David Berg who founded the Family International (formerly the Children of God).

Nevertheless, Agnieszka Pilchowa (1888–1944), one of the most celebrated of the Polish clairvoyants (deviant psychology), may be described as a hobbyist. Her uncanny ability to see events before they happened was observed in many different places and was often related to political and wartime themes prominent in the 1920s, 1930s, and early 1940s (Wikipedia, "Agnieszka Pilchowa," retrieved 30 March 2010). Her financial support came chiefly from her husband.

By contrast hobbyist individuation in deviant politics is somewhat more common than in these other two areas of deviant belief systems. Consider Ann Hansen, a Canadian anarchist. She is well-known for, among other things, her involvement in the prison abolition movement and in Direct Action, the guerrilla organization that bombed Litton Industries in 1982. She presently works as a freelance writer, having spent eight years in prison earlier in her life (Wikipedia, "Ann Hansen," retrieved 30 March 2010). In Britain, Ronnie Lee (b.1951) has been active as an anarchist since the 1970s and is especially known for his animal-rights activism and founding of the Animal Liberation Front (Wikipedia, "Ronnie Lee," retrieved 30 March 2010). Both Hansen and Lee appear to have lived for substantial parts of their anarchist careers on low incomes more or less sufficient to keep body and soul together such that they could devote many hours each day to their unconventional political interests.

CONCEIT   In chapter 2, we discussed how conceit can undermine the positive side of personal identity. In the present section we address ourselves to the twin issues of when and how conceit associated with individuation can alienate people with this disposition.

The principal alienating force where conceit is concerned is social isolation. As observed earlier with reference to conceited and individuated people, the audience finds them most disagreeable. Given this sentiment, these observers are inclined to lower their estimation of such folk. In the present section we now add that this process can foster social isolation, since few people want to hang around someone who routinely exudes vanity. Ken Keis (2010, from the Web site of CRG Consulting Resource Group; Web page no longer available) of the Educators' Resource Group inventories the costs of acting conceitedly. He presents a list of six "prices," two of which provide further detail on how such social isolation is effected:

- *In relationships* – Because they are self-centred and self-absorbed, those individuals find the needs, wants, and desires of others quite irrelevant. Confident people will avoid them.
- *In potential* – Many conceited and arrogant individuals are gifted and talented. They have simply let it go to their heads. Their challenge is that opportunities for them to grow and expand will be missed; others will avoid working with them.

Furthermore such vanity can become even more alienating when the audience looks askance at the basis for the individuation. Journalist Frank Salvato clearly disapproves of that basis in the case of Michael Vick, a well-known, individuated professional football player whom Salvato (2007) tells us had just pleaded guilty in a dogfighting scandal.

> Our society, through the ideological cancer that is moral relativism, has taken to rationalizing the cause of many a heinous act to any number of mitigating factors while excusing those who commit these acts – like Michael Vick – as victims instead of the self-centred, pampered elitists that they are. This rationalizing of purposely bad behavior facilitates a growing citizenry of conceited, entitlement-seeking malcontents who demand that they be seen, understood and accepted as correct on every issue and in every circumstance regardless of how the facts of the matter may present or

what the rules and laws mandate. The result is a society that increasingly refuses to take responsibility for its actions.

Participation

People in the process of individuating themselves through leisure participate in their communities in several ways. These ways are treated here under the headings of serious, casual, and project-based leisure and that of social capital.

SERIOUS LEISURE   Adolescent and adult men and women can distinguish themselves in certain circles – be they local, national, or international – through many of the various serious leisure activities. Thus, select athletes enjoy during their heyday the singular status of being the best amateur in their field of art, sport, science, or entertainment. Some hobbyists can achieve similar stature in, say, craftwork, collecting, mountain climbing, or barbershop singing. Such individuation can happen in volunteering when someone stands out for his or her years of dedication and imaginative service to a cause (possibly being formally recognized with one or more awards for it).

Examples abound of individuated serious leisure participants. One need only turn to the parade of gold medallists at the quadrennial summer and winter Olympic Games for a partial list of those in sport. Alan Francis stands out as holder of fifteen world titles in horseshoes, with the accompanying reputation of being the best ever in the sport (Branch 2010). In science, David Levy (astronomy) is known for his work on comets and asteroids, while Susan Hendrickson (paleontology) had a fossil dinosaur named after her. James Jackson Jarves (1818–1888), an art critic and collector, was one of the great nineteenth-century amateurs who helped develop American art collections, aesthetics, and popular interest in art history. *The Dictionary of Art Historians* (2010) holds that his most important literary work was *The Art Idea: Part Second of Confessions of an Inquirer*, published in 1864.

In the hobbyist world, Leo and Gertrude Stein gained renown for the private gallery of modern art they assembled in Paris

between 1904 and 1913. Their collection quickly gained worldwide acclaim, as did the salon and the social circle that grew up
around it. And in the hobby of ham radio, Brandon Wentworth
achieved in 1926 what was regarded at that time as the "ultimate DX" (international ham radio stations) work across all continents from his base station in California. From this event, the
first WAC (Worked All Continents) award of the International
Amateur Radio Union was born, though it was not released
until 1930 (Lombry 2010). In another hobby we find an elite
set of mountain climbers comprised of those who have scaled
the highest mountain on each of the seven continents, known in
mountaineering circles as the "seven summits." In 1985 American climber Dick Bass became the first mountaineer to climb
this group (Bass, Wells, and Ridgeway 1986). According to the
7summits.com Web page, "Statistics: Facts and Figures of all
Seven Summiteers," 199 people have achieved this distinction, as
recorded through March 2010 (retrieved 17 March 2010).

Serious leisure (or career) volunteers are most likely to gain
distinctiveness at the local level, even if some of them receive
a national or international award for their altruism there. It is
common, at least in the West, for municipal governments and
large non-profit organizations to honour one or more people
with the title of "volunteer of the year." Canada, Australia, and
New Zealand (e.g., Order of Canada, Order of Australia) give
national awards to citizens with a lifetime record of service to
their country, a service that is often of the volunteer variety and
often one carried out locally. Casual and project-based volunteers are unlikely to be recognized this way, even if they sometimes distinguish themselves in such activities.

CASUAL LEISURE   A significant amount of personal distinctiveness in casual leisure comes through being a remarkable hedon-
ist in a noteworthy sphere of everyday life. Honoured in some
circles are those (usually men) who can drink at one setting more
beer or whiskey than all other contenders (sensory stimulation
type of casual leisure). On the Guinness Book of Records Web
site, Takeru Kobayashi of Japan is held to be the fastest to eat a
12-inch pizza. He ate it in 1 minute 9.36 seconds, on 12 February

2012 (retrieved 13 February 2012). Or consider those people known in their milieu for their love of bingo, who are seemingly always at the local bingo hall (active entertainment type). As a final example, could we not describe as individuated casual leisure participants, those who are known gossips, who engage in this well-known kind of sociable conversation (discussed in chapter 2)?

Casual volunteering, though rather ordinary compared with the career variety, is nevertheless valuable activity. Thus a sort of individuation is possible here. Think of the woman who, for years, helps in the kitchen of her church to prepare food for wedding receptions, after-service gatherings, special celebrations, and the like. She eventually comes to be widely renowned in those circles for her exceptional dedication to this component of her church's mission. Or consider the man who has spent years distributing food at a local food bank, whom others in this organization recognize as the most experienced and dedicated member they have and possibly have ever seen.

PROJECT-BASED LEISURE In many cities and towns in the wintry part of North America, certain people become known for their unusually interesting exterior Christmas decorations set out around their homes. This kind of activity may be classified as occasional project-based leisure. As an example of a one-shot leisure project, let us turn again to the exalted world of conspicuous consumption, where consumers attempt to individuate themselves with extraordinary purchases:

> Noida, India – Bhisham Singh Yadav, father of the groom, is stressed. His rented Lexus got stuck behind a bullock cart. He has hired a truck to blast Hindi pop, but it is too big to maneuver through his village. At least his grandest gesture, evidence of his upward mobility, is circling overhead. The helicopter has arrived.
>
> Mr Yadav, a wheat farmer, has never flown, nor has anyone else in the family. And this will only be a short trip: delivering his son less than two miles to the village of the bride. But like many families in this expanding suburb of

New Delhi, the Yadavs have come into money, and they want everyone to know it.

"People will remember that his son went on a helicopter for his marriage," a cousin, Vikas Yadav, shouted over the din. "People should know they are spending money. For us, things like this are the stuff of dreams." (Yardley 2010)

It will be many years before Mr Yadav and his son are forgotten in the little village of Noida.

SOCIAL CAPITAL   Social capital refers to the connections among individuals, as manifested in social networks, trustworthiness, acts motivated by the norm of reciprocity, and the like (Putnam 2000). The term was coined as an analogy to the concepts of human and physical capital (e.g., natural resources, financial resources) and was based on the principle that human groups of all kinds also benefit from and advance their interests according to the salutary interconnectivity of their members.

Serious leisure generates social capital. Rojek (2002, 25) has put the case most bluntly: "Serious leisure adds to social capital through the voluntary, informal supply of caring, helping, and educative functions for the community." In support of this observation it is noteworthy that a handful of studies (for a review, see Stebbins 2007, 33) have directly focused on the question of volunteering as leisure, simultaneously viewing it both as community involvement and as a contribution to social capital.

Non-profit social entrepreneurship is an impressive example of social capital at work. Social entrepreneurs execute innovative solutions to what they define as social problems, be they local, national, or international. In social entrepreneurship, people use the principles of enterprise to foster social change, which they do by establishing and managing a venture (Light 2008, chap. 1). Some of them set up small, medium, or large non-profit groups designed to ameliorate a difficult situation threatening certain people, flora, or fauna or a certain aspect of the environment, if not a combination of these. These entrepreneurs are career volunteers, giving their time, and not infrequently their money, to start up and guide to fruition their own enterprises (Stebbins

2010a). Thus they are not as such volunteers in someone else's group or organization. This is what distinguishes the volunteering entrepreneur, since the vast majority of today's volunteers are engaged by another group or organization or, even more obscurely, work within a social movement to support a cause of some kind.

A broader contribution to the community (and sometimes even the larger society) comes from pursuing amateur and hobbyist activities as well as becoming involved in some project-based leisure. This contribution is known as "community involvement," or "civil labour." Community involvement is local voluntary activity, where members of a community participate in non-profit groups or other community work. Sometimes the goal here is to improve community life (Smith, Stebbins, and Dover 2006). Civil labour, which is nearly synonymous with community involvement, differs only in its emphasis on human activity devoted to unpaid renewal and expansion of social capital (Rojek 2002, 21). Beck (2000, 125) says that civil labour comprises housework, family work, club work, and volunteer work. This is an extremely broad conception, however, which encompasses the wide field of unpaid work, or unpaid obligation. Rojek argues, as we just noted, that for the most part, civil labour is the community contribution that amateurs, hobbyists, and career volunteers make when they pursue their serious leisure. Civil labour, however conceived of, generates social capital.

For example, Bramante (2004) describes a training project he mounted in Brazil, which he designed to stimulate civil labour among youth, thereby enabling them to contribute to their country's social capital. Youth were trained to engage in career volunteering, as both a personal and a communitarian benefit. This included: instruction on the importance of volunteers in the community, the role of art and sport there, the psychological development of the individual, the volunteer and the media, and the future of volunteering.

With one main exception casual leisure appears not to make this kind of contribution to the community. That exception is casual volunteering, during which volunteers sometimes serve with people in their community whom they would not have otherwise met (e.g., while handing out leaflets on a street corner or selling drinks at a reception). Beyond such volunteering people are sometimes joined in casual leisure with strangers, especially these days over the Internet. This also happens with tribes, that is, fragmented groupings left over from the preceding era of mass consumption, groupings recognized today by their unique tastes, lifestyles, or form of social organization. Maffesoli (1996) identifies and describes this postmodern phenomenon, which spans national borders. In this regard, he observes that mass culture has disintegrated, leaving in its wake a diversity of tribes, including the followers of heavy metal music and those youth who participate in raves. Tribes are special leisure organizations, special ways of organizing the pursuit of particular kinds of casual leisure. Tribes are also found in serious leisure, but not, however, in project-based leisure (see Stebbins 2002, 69–71).

Nevertheless some kinds of project-based leisure are capable of creating social capital. Volunteering is quite possibly the most fecund area for this, as seen in serving gratuitously at an arts festival, sports competition, or medium or large-sized conference with people not heretofore encountered. Helping preserve human life or wildlife after a natural or human-made disaster caused by, for instance, a hurricane, earthquake, oil spill, or industrial accident is normally carried out with other people, many or all of whom were strangers before. Finally, in the area of entertainment and theatre, participants are usually in a position to meet members of the audience and organizers of the event when they present a public talk or perform in, or work backstage for, a community pageant.

How often does this kind of activity lead to personal individuation? We know of no research that can answer this question with empirical data. Still it is certainly conceivable that individuals could distinguish themselves, for example, by the exceptional quality of their involvement, amount of time devoted to the activity, or emotional dedication to it. Could not a person be recognized among the other volunteers for his or her remarkable efforts to save shore birds following an oil spill? Sometimes people, even though they do not routinely perform as such, give a moving public talk, for which they are remembered for some time. David Gergen (2006) discusses several social entrepreneurs who have individuated themselves by creating successful non-profit enterprises organized around solving an important social problem. Nonetheless the possibility of individuation in tribes seems to be stifled by their "collective consciousness" (*conscience collective*; Maffesoli 1996, 76), though chiefly for taste-based as opposed to activity-based tribes (Stebbins 2002, 65–71).

The foregoing discussion of the link between social capital, serious leisure, and individuation runs counter to Robert Putnam's conclusions on the matter:

> The most commonly cited weakness of "Bowling Alone" had been clear to me from the start – by drawing primarily on evidence about declining membership in specific formal groups, I had ignored the possibility of offsetting increases in other groups or in informal types of connectedness. For some alleged counterexamples, like soccer matches and football and softball games, hard work unearthed hard evidence, and they turned out mostly to be illusory, but that momentary clarification left undiminished the possibility that other over-looked forms of social capital were expanding. I simply could think of no source of systematic evidence on civic engage-ment in general, and still less on such ephemera as picnics and card games. My colleagues Kristin Goss and Steve Yonish spent hundreds of hours in endlessly resourceful (but usually fruitless) searches for systematic evidence of what we called "unobtrusive indicators" of social connectedness. (Putnam 2000, 508)

Putnam goes on to discuss additional archival data that support "massively" his claims for "civic disengagement."

Putnam's work notwithstanding there is evidence, most of it qualitative, that social capital can flow from participation in serious leisure. Since publication of his book, *Bowling Alone: The Collapse and Revival of American Community*, it has become possible to measure, quantitatively, serious and casual leisure (Gould et al. 2008; Tsaur and Liang 2008). Quantitative measurement of the social capital potential of serious leisure should provide needed light on this obscure area of the bowling alone thesis.

CITIZENSHIP

Next we look at the relationship of individuation and citizenship. Margaret Somers defines citizenship as: "a personal political status rooted in a set of universal rights that are enforceable by claims on the state and, historically, founded on the legal necessities of capitalist society and its government. Membership, participation, association, inclusion/exclusion, national identity, and the rule of law number among the core components of citizenship" (Somers 1993, 558 and 594). Sometimes referred to as "active citizenship," this conceptualization includes not only rights but also responsibilities, commonly understood as feeling obliged to work toward improving community life. Although such improvement can be carried out in either work or leisure, we will in this section consider only its leisure expression. Consonant with the discussion of obligation in leisure presented in chapter 2, obligation in citizen responsibility to be felt as leisure must also be seen as agreeable. It is not, in these activities, a nonwork obligation.

Here, too, the review is mixed, in that some kinds of distinctiveness are inimical to universal rights and responsibilities, whereas others harmonize with, if not support, these two. Our concern in this section is with how individuated performances in amateur, hobbyist, and volunteer activities and in leisure projects contribute to the support of such rights and responsibilities. We approach this question by examining how leisure fosters individuation through social capital, communal projects, communal values (cultural [art, science, sport, entertainment, hobbies], political, economic), and social well-being. We also consider how personal distinctiveness can undermine these sources of citizenship.

Social Capital

In the preceding section we explored how community participation through leisure generates social capital. The question to be examined in this section is where and how such participation results in individual distinctiveness while also serving as evidence of citizenship.

Individuation along the lines of being a good citizen rests on exceptional discharge of communal responsibilities. One of the examples given in the final paragraph of the preceding section exemplifies individuated citizenship achieved during leisure: the person recognized among the other volunteers for his or her remarkable efforts to save shore birds following an oil spill. Another instance could be the amateur athlete, say, an Olympic medal winner, who gains further recognition by visiting patients at a children's hospital, or a school principal who comes to be recognized for establishing a social enterprise designed to teach youngsters and teenagers to write essays and short stories and to foster an enduring interest in these activities. In all three examples the responsibilities of citizenship are met through volunteer activities, culminating in a significant measure of distinctive community recognition. At the same time social capital is generated when these individuated people rub elbows with others in the community whom they did not know or had little to do with earlier.

Communal Projects

Communal projects are undertakings, public or private, that when finished produce a lasting benefit for all or part of a community. By "community" we mean a town or city, an ethnic group, a neighbourhood, a taste group (e.g., baseball fans, nature lovers, consumers of fine art), and the like. The question explored in this section is, "How might a person become individuated through involvement in a leisure activity that both contributes to a communal project and meets the responsibilities of citizenship?"

Conceiving of and setting in motion the steps needed to bring such a project to fruition is a typical way to individuate oneself. To the extent that it solves or helps solve a social problem, the initiator of a communal project is a social entrepreneur. The social entrepreneurial person stands out as the one who started up, for instance, a needed shelter for the homeless, service for drug addicts, or centre for newcomers to the city. Beyond the sphere of social entrepreneurship people may become known for taking the initiative to, say, form a softball league, organize a book exchange service, or establish a social club. These latter projects are not, however, tackled in the hope of solving a social problem (a necessary precondition of a social enterprise), but rather to meet a particular community need. In all these examples, as in many other instances of individuation, the breadth of the individuated person's reputation may be highly varied. Thus, the reputation of the woman who sets up the shelter for homeless people would probably be wider than that of the man who forms the small social club.

People may also come to be well-known for their contributions to communal projects which someone else initiated and for which that person possibly gained a fair amount of local acclaim. So Mr Jones establishes a softball league and, during the next few years, directs its operations. Following his retirement from this responsibility, Ms Brown takes over directorship of the league. Her ability at raising funds results in a solid financial foundation, a rare asset for a non-profit group and a capacity that Jones lacked. Ms Brown soon gains significant admiration in softball circles for her fund-raising acumen. Similar possibilities for individuation await highly regarded leaders of social enterprises who make unique contributions to these organizations, even though they did this many years after the organizations were founded.

To the extent that communal projects advance by way of the leisure efforts of individuals, it is the volunteering type that is by far the most common here. Moreover, as far as individuation is concerned, career volunteering is the primary route for this distinction. Of course casual volunteers also play an important role in communal projects of all sorts, but there appears to be little opportunity to acquire significant individuation by serving in this capacity.

Communal Values

Values are a society's idea of what is good and desirable; the good and the desirable satisfy a collective need or desire. Since almost anything can be valued by members of society, we will limit our discussion to those values capable of promoting or undermining individuated citizenship. To this end, we will consider the communal values of success, achievement, freedom of action, individual personality, and activity (being involved in something), all taken from a larger list of American values set out by Williams (2000, 146). Then we look at social well-being, treated here as an overarching communal value. People experience social well-being once they realize the preceding five values. Other values from Williams's inventory might be examined, but the set selected here is sufficient to demonstrate how values, leisure, citizenship, and individuation are closely intertwined.

Within the domain of free time, people are most likely to realize in serious leisure one or more of the values just listed and, to a lesser extent, do this in project-based leisure. Here, for instance, as members of a community orchestra they succeed in providing classical music to the town, which is an achievement that allows them freedom of artistic expression by means of a respected activity. Furthermore the players enjoy the uncommon social identity of belonging to this orchestra, while a few of them may be individuated through exposure of their exceptional musical talent (primarily through well-executed solos). Citizenship is expressed in this example, as measured by its components of membership, participation, association, and inclusion.

Consider another example, this time from the world of hobbies, featuring local model railroaders who occasionally mount for popular consumption exhibitions of the fruits of their pastime. A successful exhibition is an achievement. There is significant freedom in how to mount the display such that it is both pleasing and informative for observers. Like the classical music orchestra, model railroading is a respectable pursuit. And, since a very small proportion of the population goes in for this activity, those who engage in it enjoy a special social identity. An individuated model railroader would likely be someone who has created an especially elaborate display at home, who has tirelessly promoted the hobby for years, who has an enviable collection of trains, and the like. Here, as in the classical music orchestra, citizenship is expressed in the components of membership, participation, association, and inclusion.

Many leisure projects are capable of realizing the same values and manifesting citizenship in the same way as the serious leisure activities. By contrast casual leisure participants realize fewer of these values. At times tribalized consumption by modern youth does lead to individualization of personality, as through participation in one of the tribes discussed earlier in this chapter. Furthermore, choosing a casual leisure activity does evince a certain freedom of action, and the chooser does thereby get involved in something. But, in so doing, this person is not, at least while engaged in the chosen casual leisure activity, also realizing the values of success, achievement, and – outside the tribal world – individual personality. From the standpoint of communal values sought within the domain of free time, casual leisure, compared with the other two forms, offers the weakest access to them.

Social Well-Being

Keyes (1998, 121) defines social well-being as the "absence of negative conditions and feelings, the result of adjustment and adaptation to a hazardous world." For him well-being, though a personal state, is influenced by many of the social conditions considered earlier and incorporated in the serious leisure perspective. Though the relationship is probably more complex than this, for purposes of the present discussion let us incorporate in the following proposition what has been said to this point in this section: social well-being emanates from a high quality of life, as generated by some combination of serious leisure balanced with one or both of the other two forms.

Our sense of being a citizen is itself an element in our social well-being, for this state is achieved, among other ways, through the six components mentioned earlier: membership, participation, association, inclusion/exclusion, national identity, and the rule of law. Still the relationship of citizenship and well-being is reciprocal, in that the latter helps make people good citizens. Diener and Tov (2007), in their study of social well-being, found that it varies widely across nations. They observed that, in general, it is associated with confidence in government and the armed forces, emphasis on post-materialist values, support for democracy, lowered intolerance of immigrants and racial groups, among other factors. An elevated sense of social well-being, the authors concluded, correlates strongly with peaceful attitudes. Their results attest to the strong reciprocity between well-being and citizenship.

But can people become individuated by dint of their personal well-being? Here, too, we run up against a lack of data on this issue. Nevertheless the answer to this question is, conceivably, yes. Do we not know people who seem exceptionally well-adjusted, exceptionally at ease with themselves and their lot in daily life? Individuals who stand out against a background of other people we know whose well-being is significantly compromised by one or more critical conditions, exemplified in tension at work, marital disharmony, poor health, lack of fulfillment in leisure, and political anger. Leisure, although highly important as a source of well-being, is still only one of several such sources, which means that further inquiry into individuation by way of exceptional well-being would take us beyond the range of this book.

GLOBALIZATION

Globalization is defined here as the tendency toward internationalization of ideas, practices, artifacts, and so forth, whether their worldwide spread at this time is either still partial or now more or less complete. The question pursued in this section is how does the individualized person fit with this tendency? In many ways globalization fosters worldwide homogenization of personalities, activities, patterns of thought, and the like. At the same time the would-be individualized person has the opportunity to cut an extraordinary figure on this bland international stage. In particular we explore in this section, as an extension of the earlier section on participation, the possibilities existing in our globalized world for people whose individuality rests on their achievements in serious leisure and devotee work (e.g., as artists, athletes, scientists, entertainers, volunteers, and social entrepreneurs). From what we have been able to observe, the other two forms of leisure offer few opportunities of this nature.

Serious Leisure

In this section attention will be for the most part on more or less contemporary instances of individuation in the four types of serious leisure. It is easy to find examples of famous amateurs back in history, before these areas professionalized, and a number of those amateurs enjoyed national, if not international, reputations in their field of expertise. But globalization is at its greatest expanse today, which has not, however, discouraged individuation at this level. That said, some of the examples in this section feature people whose reputations are primarily national or regional (several nations). And a few became famous in the nineteenth century. Finally, in this review, we have intentionally eschewed people largely celebrated for other reasons than their amateur activities (e.g., American President Dwight Eisenhower as amateur painter, Benjamin Franklin as amateur scientist). In this kind of work-leisure relationship, it is difficult to disentangle the global reach of the two domains, because the enormous prominence of the work role of such personages tends to valorize the public image of their leisure roles and activities.

Let us turn first to globalized individuation through art as a leisure activity. For example, Alexander Borodin (1833–1887), a successful chemist and physician, was also a world-renowned amateur composer of classical music. Borodin was a member of the group based in Saint Petersburg called "the Five"; it included composers Nikolai Rimsky-Korsakov and Modest Mussorgsky, who became world famous amateurs at a time when professional composers were also working. Much more recently, the June 2009 edition of the *Hanoi Grapevine* publicized a concert in the Concert Hall of the Hanoi University of Culture. It featured a number of famous amateur singers (famous in Vietnam) presenting the songs of composer Trinh Cong Son. And for a third illustration we draw on Vello Õnnis (b.1938), a well-known amateur artist in Saaremaa, Estonia. As a trained mariner by profession, it is not surprising perhaps that Õnnis incorporates maritime themes in his paintings. The Estonian Embassy in Riga, Latvia, exhibited in 2009 a selection of his paintings.

Prominent among the set of globally distinguished amateur scientists is Grote Reber (1911–2002), a pioneer of radio astronomy. He was trained in radio engineering in the United States and had a parallel passion for ham radio. He was thus inspired to construct several radio telescopes, an advanced version of which was capable of receiving signals from outer space. By the age of fifteen he had also built his own radio set and had become a "ham" operator. Karl Jansky's (1905–1950) discovery in 1933 of radio noise from outer space inspired Reber to further the work on his own (Madehow.com 2010). In fact, Reber presents a textbook case of the amateur-to-professional leisure/work career: an amateur whose leisure passion spurs him on to a school-based training program after which he becomes a devotee professional (Stebbins 2004a, 73–4).

Discover Magazine (e.g., Schlesinger 2008) contains short entries on several scientific amateurs with globalized reputations in their area of expertise. For example, in June 2008, David Gowen, an outdoor enthusiast and retired carpenter, discovered two new, related wild flowers of the phlox family growing in the Walnut Creek area of California. In amateur paleontology Stephen Felton, a contractor, stands out for his work on Ordovician fossils (i.e., snails). He was honoured in 2001 by the Paleontological Society, one of the world's leading scientific societies devoted to the study of fossils. And Ron Bissinger, a CEO of a life sciences company, has a world reputation for his work on detecting exoplanets, or those planets that orbit distant stars.

Amateur athletes are individuated, in part, through highly visible sponsorships by commercial interests and, in part, through their achievements in their sport. We have already commented on the fame such participation can bring. What remains now is to observe the universality of fame acquired from winning in international competitions (especially the Olympic Games) and contests and the opportunities for endorsing worldwide products that sometimes follow.

But global individuation can also bring trouble. High visibility flowing from outstanding athletic success and commercial promotion also brings high public scrutiny for possible moral lapses. That is, given today's popular fascination with scandals among the rich and famous, the famous athlete must avoid being discovered engaging in questionable activities or appearing to have done this. Thus, McCarthy (2010) writes:

> With the 2010 Vancouver Games completed, the competition has begun for endorsement gold. And [golfer] Tiger Woods' loss could be an Olympian's gain.
>
> Woods' stunning fall from corporate grace could boost the prospects of the most marketable Winter Olympians, sports marketers say. Among the potential winners: the USA's Shaun White, Lindsey Vonn, Apolo Anton Ohno, Julia Mancuso, Shani Davis, Bode Miller and Evan Lysacek; Canada's Sidney Crosby and Joannie Rochette; and South Korea's Kim Yu-Na.
>
> Only a few Olympians pick up big-money deals after a Games. The rest are usually ignored by Madison Avenue until they are preparing to compete four years later.
>
> But the sex scandal embroiling Woods is adding a new dynamic. Woods has been dumped by Gatorade, AT&T and Accenture. His problems could make marketers pass on mainstream athletes and hire Olympians, who are seen as safer bets, although swimming star Michael Phelps, for example, was photographed smoking a marijuana pipe.

Remember, however, that not every sport is equally endorsable. For example, curling and the equestrian sports have much less commercial appeal than snowboarding and swimming.

In amateur entertainment it is not uncommon to get a start by performing during "amateur nights" on a local stage. Stand-up comedy institutionalized these events decades ago in what is often called "open mic," or "amateur," night. It typically takes place during an early- or mid-week evening, where anyone can mount the stage with five to ten minutes of (hopefully) humorous material (Stebbins 1990, 22–3). The Apollo Theater in New

York City operates along similar lines. It has been in business under that name since 1934, hosting each year a huge variety of amateur musical, singing, dance, and comedic acts. A number of its performers have subsequently gained considerable renown as professionals (e.g., in music, Ella Fitzgerald, Benny Carter, Stevie Wonder, and Michael Jackson). Our interest here, however, is not in their kind of professional success, but rather in the success of those artists who become famous while still amateurs, in Apollo's case as a result of placing first, second, or even third in its annual Super Dog competition. In the twenty-first century this theatre has served as the model for other breeding grounds of celebrated amateurs, most notably *American Idol* and *So You Think You Can Dance*. In all these programs and shows, winning contestants enjoy individuation in that leisure status. Nonetheless their elevated standing will be short-lived should they become professionals in their art, for the public, enthralled as it is with professional entertainment, is inclined to forget about its less glamorous precursors.

CONCLUSION

This chapter, with its emphasis on context, may have created the impression that individuation in leisure and devotee work is mostly a "big time" matter. That individuated people in this domain of life usually have reputations of national or international scope. Still we have also presented numerous examples of individuated locals, people who stand out for their accomplishments in their town or city. In other words, individuation is about being a big frog, either in a small pond or a large one.

Additionally this chapter raises the question of whether people individuated through serious leisure, project-based leisure, or devotee work have sought this reputation. In chapter 2 we discussed the intense intrinsic appeal of such activity – that pursuing it constitutes its principal reward. This part of the serious leisure perspective suggests, then, that individuation is a by-product, something that is nice but relatively superficial compared with the powerful rewards experienced in doing the core activity itself. In support of this explanation, note that the fourth reward – self-image – in the list of ten in chapter 2 (p. 42) has in research studies always been ranked well below the first three and often below the social rewards 8 through 10 (Stebbins 2007, 14). From the evidence at hand we may then say that an individuated reputation in complex leisure and devotee work is not usually a goal – by contrast to casual leisure, where standing out in some hedonic way *is* a central motivator.

All this is not to argue, however, that once the fact of individuation wins its own appeal, the participant whose reputation is expanding is oblivious to this personal transformation in the public eye. It is even conceivable that the individual's reputation could become a dominant, even the dominant, reward, possibly eclipsing or at least diminishing ones like self-enrichment, self-actualization, and self-expression. Indeed getting known is a vital strategy in the entertainment world, which may entail accepting performance opportunities that are rather disagreeable (returning few if any of the ten rewards) but felt to be necessary for career advancement.

This version of selling one's soul to the devil should not be overlooked in our quest to present a balanced picture of individuation in all its respects, positive and negative. In the meantime, remember that most amateurs, participants in leisure projects, and devotee workers experience little or no significant individuation. They love what they do chiefly for the fulfillment it brings. For them no other rewards are needed.

These six main chapters have examined individuality from several angles, philosophical, sociological, person-centred, and contextual, all within the framework of the serious leisure perspective. From this broad appreciation of the whys and wherefores of distinctiveness, several issues have come to the fore. They are treated in the concluding chapter of this book.

Conclusion

Six issues have emerged out of the ferment of the preceding chapters, which will become the centre of attention in this, the final chapter. They are (1) How does achieved individuality relate to ascribed – sometimes, inherited – individuality? (2) How important is it to be distinctive and therefore not part of what David Riesman (1961) called the "lonely crowd"? (3) What is the difference in being an individual for reasons of ascription vis-à-vis those of achievement? (4) Should everyone strive for individuality beyond that already allotted to them by nature? (5) How does leisure space offer individuals significant opportunities to pursue their deep aspiration to be who they really are? and (6) What is the role of leisure education in empowering people toward unique individuality and thereby avoiding the trap of individualism's abyss? We will apply ourselves to these issues in order.

ISSUE 1: ACHIEVED AND ASCRIBED INDIVIDUALITY

The concepts of "ascribed" and "achieved" entered sociology by way of Ralph Linton (1936), an anthropologist. He applied them to the various statuses people hold in a society, noting that these statuses are subject to evaluation, collective judgments that eventually find their place in the social hierarchy. He observed that people attain statuses in two main ways: by achievement and by ascription. The first requires personal effort, the outcome of which can be seen in, for example, educational diplomas, annual income, and organizational membership. Ascription, by contrast, is based on the personal characteristics that we are born with or otherwise have thrust upon us, for example age, sex, ethnicity, and in some countries, religion. Some statuses, whether ascribed or achieved, have a high evaluation (e.g., being born into the royal family, becoming a medical doctor), while others are low (e.g., being born female in a traditional Islamic community, being sentenced for a criminal act).

Much of the individuality discussed in the preceding chapters appears to result in an achieved status of some kind. The distinguished painter and athlete are well-known examples. So is the community volunteer whose amount and quality of service stands out from that of other local volunteers. Instances of distinguished ascribed statuses are, however, more difficult to find. Besides being born into a royal family, ascribed distinctiveness could come from gaining significant inherited wealth in the form of property or money, having certain remarkable physical characteristics (e.g., the world's tallest man, the person with the longest tongue, or the individual having the most fingers and toes), or coming into a significant family hand-me-down like an outstanding collection of coins or old cars or a rare painting or musical instrument.

In harmony with the scope of this book, note that achieved and ascribed statuses are by no means always aligned with leisure interests. If the heir of a coin collection wants to continue expanding the collection, this person has been handed an interesting hobby complete with the renown enjoyed earlier by the donor. Still mere possession of a rare painting is not itself a leisure activity, nor is being exceptionally tall or being born into a royal family. Nonetheless viewing social life through the lens of achieved and ascribed statuses does show that the study of individuality is not confined to the boundaries of leisure space. In fact a most prominent example of its extension beyond leisure is individuality in the workplace, even if much of that individuality springs from devotee work. Furthermore it is possible for achieved and ascribed statuses to change within a person's lifetime. For instance many an athlete must face physical decline and with it a new status (now one that is ascribed) of former tennis or basketball player. Even certain kinds of ascribed individuality may be modified, as when the royal family falls from grace or one of its members renounces his or her place in it. Or an heir to a valuable and distinctive collection could decide to sell it, losing thereby that basis for ascriptive distinctiveness.

ISSUE 2: THE IMPORTANCE OF DISTINCTIVENESS

David Riesman (1961) held that, at the time he was writing about American society, many of its members were in danger of being swept into the "lonely crowd." He qualified these people as "other-directed":

> What is common to all the other-directed people is that their contemporaries are the source of direction for the individual – either those known to him or those with whom he is indirectly acquainted, through friends and through the mass media. This source is of course "internalized" in the sense that dependence on it for guidance in life is implanted early. The goals toward which the other-directed person strives shift with that guidance: it is only the process of striving itself and the process of paying close attention to the signals from others that remain unaltered throughout life. (21)

Riesman speculated that other-directed Americans had an enduring need for approval, a main differentiating characteristic. He contrasted this type with the inner-directed person, someone whose social gyroscope is "implanted early in life by the elders and directed toward generalized but nonetheless inescapably destined goals" (15). There is in this type a sense of the driven workaholic (popular sense of the word; see Stebbins 2004a, 28–9). The "tradition-directed" type, the third in Riesman's tripartite typology, was the tradition-directed person, for whom the tribe, clan, and village constituted main bases for this dominant orientation to life.

Riesman wrote over sixty years ago (the first edition of *The Lonely Crowd* was published in 1950), at a time when Americans could be interpreted as becoming more and more other-directed and the other two types were fading into oblivion. Moreover, based on what will be said shortly, we may conclude that other-direction is still with us today. Meanwhile neither inner-direction nor tradition-direction seems to have gained any ground. Note, too, that the inner-directed type fails to conform even reasonably to our conception of a person individuated in leisure, for the latter marches substantially to his or her own tune (not one set by their elders) and is more or less oblivious to the larger, other-directed lonely crowd.

That is, most of the people about whom we have written earlier are not oriented by inescapable, predestined goals that animate their pursuit of distinctiveness. They have too much autonomy for that, a point made by McClay (2009) about the absence of such in Riesman`s description of the inner-directed type. Riesman himself, in an article published in 1990, commented on this deficiency:

> The notion of "autonomy" was rather thinly sketched [in *The Lonely Crowd*]. As it was interpreted by many readers, it proved to be at best an ambiguous and at worst a harmful ideal. Individuals seeking to show that they were not "other-directed," that they were unconstrained by parents or peers found extravagant ways to flaunt their supposed authenticity. The wish to exhibit autonomy or authenticity strengthened the cult of candor. In a new hypocrisy we disguised even from ourselves our virtuous selves, our impulses of caring and concern toward others. (Quoted in McClay 2009, 27)

The individuated participant in leisure activities is not substantially other-directed, however common this type is today in the United States and elsewhere. This participant, who really amounts to a fourth type, is, however, often distinction-directed, in the sense conveyed through Bourdieu's (1979) concept of distinction. This classification of the individuated participant is explained in the next section.

ISSUE 3: REASONS FOR BECOMING INDIVIDUATED

We argued in chapter 2 that it is possible to become individuated through any of the three forms of leisure, and that casual leisure offers the fewest opportunities for such transformation. The preceding discussion about ascribed and achieved statuses bears this out. Because they are accidents of birth, marriage, inheritance, or gift giving, our ascribed statuses mostly just fall, as it were, into our lap. True, certain gifts and inheritances might be steered to the recipient or heir because this person has succeeded in persuading the giver to act accordingly. Yet such cases appear to be exceptions to the rule. They are, moreover, relatively uncommon occurrences in life, especially for those statuses regarded in the community as distinctive. In short, one might want to become individuated by way of ascription, but most of the time, it will be necessary to wait for this to happen. And in any case, gaining ascribed distinctiveness is uncommon.

We do not wish to imply that achieved individuality is the main reason or even a reason at all for engaging in a serious or project-based leisure activity leading to this status. Such activities are intrinsically appealing, highly absorbing, and bring about varying degrees of self-fulfillment. That the participant becomes renowned in certain circles for exceptional accomplishments in the activity is, in the typical instance, most gratifying, but for all that hardly the main reason for pursuing it.

In other words, some achieved individuality is external, or extrinsic, in that public recognition is its basis. Internal, or intrinsic, achieved individuality, on the other hand, is the person's own sense of being distinctive for a particular achievement or set of achievements. It is a kind of inner recognition of having realized through considerable effort a deep and long-felt aim.

Nonetheless, once distinctiveness has been reached and the distinguished person recognizes this new external and internal evaluation of his or herself, that evaluation may then become a prominent value worth pursuing. It is at this point in the leisure career where the distinction-directed person typically gets fired up by the fact of his own renown. For people thus individualized the challenge now is how to deal gracefully with their newfound prominence. In this respect we explained in chapter 2 how conceit can undermine the positive side of individual identity. Instead humility and modesty were said to be the more agreeable approaches to socially managing distinctiveness, with the second being more palatable to the general public than the first. In sum, individuation as a reason for becoming individuated in serious and project-based leisure arrives quite late in the game, but once there it poses a problem for distinctive people in how to present themselves publicly with proper decorum.

This said, ascribed distinctiveness, when it occurs, has an unmistakable clarity about it. You are or are not born as royalty, you receive an identity-enhancing gift or inheritance or you fail to, and so on. Not so with achieved distinctiveness accomplished as it is with great effort, perseverance, creativity, or innovation. Achieved statuses take many months, usually many years, to develop. A person's identity as someone distinctive, as someone who has earned this communal image through effort, perseverance, and the like, is an often surprising result of a slowly unfolding process.

ISSUE 4: SHOULD EVERYONE STRIVE FOR INDIVIDUALITY BEYOND THAT ALREADY ALLOTTED?

To build our genuine individuality demands, as we just said, effort and perseverance. We are generally more motivated to concentrate all our means and efforts to realize some special and exceptional mission or event limited in time, rather than undertake a sustained effort for an extended time. As an example, a couple may invest their combined resources, or even some of their future incomes, to have the greatest wedding, but forget that the main purpose of their marriage would be to renew, day after day, the vitality and the justification of their shared life. Achieving genuine individuality through dynamic and changing circumstances demands, then, a lifelong endeavour.

It is easier of course to continue with what we have "gained": the identity that the given circumstances of life have given us, a disparate set of attributes through which we are recognized by others and through which we also see ourselves. This is the external image, the official identity, and the few familiar social roles we play to ensure our legitimate existence among others. To see this more clearly, it is helpful to distinguish, as González Pecotche (1998) has suggested, between "personality" and "individuality," with personality being this external image we try to "sell" to the others, an image of which we are the principal buyers. The main preoccupation is to appear to others in some way – a preoccupation greatly exploited for marketing in our consumer culture, where we are invited to enhance our appearance with the most recent trendy labels.

We do sense sometimes a kind of divorce, a gap between those we believe we are, and also want others to believe we are, and the deep inner self – a gap stressed by the vain race against the latest model, the trendiest label. In today's world, we must also add the unease which comes from the instability of almost any criterion we once attached to self-identity, such as professional function, membership in a defined community, and so on. In time, individuals discover how fragile is an allotted individuality – i.e., "personality," in the terminology of González Pecotche. They weary of the demands of maintaining an image and feel the need of something more genuine and serene. They understand that they should strive for personal uniqueness, beyond changing circumstances and fleeting trends. This demands of course, not only determination, perseverance, and effort, but also a privileged space apart from the arena of daily survival, a space like the leisure realm.

ISSUE 5: LEISURE SPACE AS A SECOND CHANCE

With the end of the world of unreflective mediocrity, everyone has to find his or her own way through the cacophony of innumerable social and moral messages, wrapped up in a sometimes explicit, but mostly hidden, social harassment. Nobody is safe; even traditional communities are infiltrated and their leaders engage in hard, continuous work to try to fill the fissures.

Nowadays it's quite impossible to escape from freedom. Life is no longer the small grocery totally dominated by the grocer, keeping all his cherished merchandise behind the counter. Life is a completely open supermarket, offering an unlimited variety of suggestions and temptations. People are there, alone with their envies, their necessities, their weaknesses, and their lack of preparedness to choose and be entirely responsible for their choices. Nothing can save them, not even modular conformism, with its ephemeral illusion that acting like the many others will reduce each one's accountability. Each of us has to accept the challenge of being something, that is, of realizing our personal freedom.

And if acting differently, if acting independently of the role we are expected to play, is highly risky, then leisure could be an easy and friendly space for learning to deal with one's freedom without any risk, or at least with very little of it. Leisure is by its nature a break from day-to-day tasks, during which we have the legitimacy to do whatever we choose, even if only choosing not to choose. Leisure space is an extraterritorial domain, a vast workshop in which one can discover, try, adopt, and create for the sake of discovering, trying, and creating in harmony with one's nascent uniqueness, beyond the daily necessities and social obligations.

There, leisure experience may enable us to encounter new fields of interest that may echo with aspirations lying deep within us throughout most of our lives. More, we will use unknown talents that have remained ignored because they were irrelevant to the expected performances of customary life. We will then have surpassed leisure as entertainment and distraction. We will be in the presence of leisure as a valuable opportunity to find the best materials and the best ways to express one's essential linkage with life, that is, with all its rich and innumerable expressions.

In the free space of leisure and during its free time, one has a second and vital opportunity to really be a genuine and unique self, "the real being, the hidden one, the individual, the inner being, the living spirit within oneself" (González Pecotche 1998, 401). To undertake such a process, the individual has to be restored. People can learn how to play as a whole in the whole of life, a life much more rich and significant than the depleted life of a "buyer" in the mega-mall of the worldwide market economy. To step into leisure's open fields demands its own training, its specific education.

Individuality in Modern Thought

Before proceeding to discuss issue 6, since the five issues just presented all bear on agency and structure, this is a good point at which to situate our treatment of individuality within some of the intellectual debate on these two aspects over the past half century. This digression will be superficial, however, for a full treatment of the place of the ideas presented in this book within the larger world of thought on individuality would be complicated enough to warrant a separate book-length publication. That is, it is enough to set out and interrelate in one volume our ideas and observations as they have emerged from philosophy, sociology, and leisure studies.

Earlier we alluded to some of this literature – it is largely concerned with individualism rather than individuality – but we now need to say a bit more about the agency/structure debate, in which this book certainly has a place. Anthony Giddens (1986), for example, incorporates both structure and agency in his theory of structuration, a stance on the question that resembles in many ways Pierre Bourdieu's (1977) approach. Our analysis of individuality squares with the thoughts of both men, though this book leans more toward the agency end of the scale. Still, chapter 6 was meant to place our earlier argument in context in the social structure, in the constraints and opportunities that people find in community, and in the various organizations they deal with as they pursue their individuating interests. Our definition of agency was presented in chapter 2, as the second step in setting one's self apart from others by following the road to leisure.

Our discourse on individuality can also be situated in Jürgen Habermas's (1985) theory of communicative action. People searching for distinctiveness do so in line with his unique definition of rationality. For Habermas, rationality is both subjective and practical, consisting mainly of the ways people, as they speak and act, acquire and use knowledge, demonstrating in the process that they are knowledgeable actors. As such they can interact effectively, or practically, with other knowledgeable actors, the result being for some people that they set themselves on a course leading to distinctiveness.

Another fruitful contextual angle on individuality was pursued by Bourdieu (1979), who noted that the amounts and types of people's cultural capital determine their relative status in a given field. In education, for example, upper-class students enjoy different forms of such capital, giving them an advantage over those of lower-class origin. Fields become, as it were, battlefields, on which there occur struggles to improve personal status and define what counts as a legitimate or recognized achievement. Bourdieu observed that, in the artistic field, avant-garde artists are faced with the task of trying to establish their own definition of art vis-à-vis the establishment's.

Surely, a thoroughgoing analysis of the search for distinctiveness framed in the agency/structure debate would enhance substantially our understanding of both of these scholarly fields.

ISSUE 6: THE ROLE OF LEISURE EDUCATION

Ingrid Betancourt, in her recent book (2010) telling of her captivity, wrote: "pushed by the most shameful humiliation, I preserved though the most valuable freedom which nobody would ever take away, the freedom to decide who I wanted to be" (from the back cover). This is a wonderful account of a great realization of the human prerogative in an extreme circumstance. It reminds us once more that people are not preprogrammed but always have the prerogative to decide how to relate to every circumstance. Of course there are influences, sometimes very heavy and decisive, but nonetheless we all have the last say, even if that last say is one of silence. Any act, any word pronounced by me, is a tacit decision of who I decide to be.

We can of course see Ingrid Betancourt and many others as superhuman and fly to the shelter of mediocrity where most people are, where there are apparently no choices, where we can dissolve our responsibility, being only one of the masses. Yet, whether conscious of it or not, you are the sole author of your life. You can collaborate with the normalizing forces of society and decide to be "normal," an average passive spectator of the superhuman, or see, by contrast, in every human deed something properly human and then decide whether it is proper to one's self. The individual is free, then, to be inspired and to decide whether to improve himself. That is our great prerogative to undertake to improve our capacities and to aspire to elevate ourselves above the common and mediocre, the virtual and imaginary average: the prerogative to be oneself.

As we have said in all the previous chapters of this book, leisure can offer this special break within the stressing struggle for survival, a break where we can re-encounter ourselves and the unlimited perspectives available to us in which to realize our uniqueness. However, entering into the realm of leisure, not as a mere distraction but as an opportunity to strive for individuality beyond "personality" shaped by obligations, needs, and external circumstances demands a new kind of training. Here we discover that the social game is not enough – we need to be initiated into another dimension of existence.

Leisure education means a serious rehearsal for a new kind of game of life. Within this endeavour, the aims of education itself will have changed: we will no longer be looking for ways to achieve something *in* life, but aspire to achieve life itself, a life with all angles considered, life with its innumerable facets, phases, and possibilities. In this sense, the leisure state of mind invites us, not only to consume, to copy, to reproduce – but to create. Through a continuous process of serious self-development, we come to discern the intuited nuances of our emerging individuality. We learn more and more about ourselves. Thanks to creative experiences, free of any instrumentality, we begin to hear more and more of the subtle notes of our sensitivity, and become better listeners to all of what that sensitivity gathers up, and we improve our ability to decipher, to understand, and to adjust our self-concepts to our genuine, essential nature.

Leisure education implies a serious self-development, open to various new dimensions, and essentially leads into the realm of artistic creation. Like art, leisure is the domain of freedom, of personal choices between innumerable possibilities. Step by step, a new individuality grows and becomes present in all the domains of life. Step by step, we draw together the inner harmony of our uniqueness, which will be recognizable whenever and wherever we will be – that is, we will act, we will express our personal choices. Leisure education is also an essential training for an open dialogue with life. "Education, inspired by the value of freedom, must offer the concepts and principles that enable individuals to conduct this dialog between their interior selves and the larger world and thereby increase their individuality. Only this individuality can create an authentic relationship with life that will be fuller and richer in its content than before, because this life delves deeper, far deeper than appearances" (Cohen-Gewerc and Stebbins 2007, 45).

Let us remember all the individuals, all the groups, who struggle often at the risk of their lives for the recognition of humanity as individual, as individuality. We should try to make ourselves deserving of this great inheritance by realizing this essential prerogative reconquered by their courage and sacrifice: the prerogative to be ourselves.

To be oneself means not to be dissolved in the mass, shaped by ongoing circumstances. To be oneself means to be aware of one's individuality and conscious of one's presence in a fascinating dialogue with the world – a dialogue that is the sole way to improve and empower our uniqueness, our individuality, and thereby avoid the trap of individualism's abyss.

Notes

INTRODUCTION

1 John McFarland Kennedy, trans. (Nietzsche 1911).
2 Inspired by the French *noblesse oblige*!

CHAPTER ONE

1 In Hebrew "freedom" is used as a synonym for vacations or holidays.
2 See chapter 2.
3 See the play *No Exit* by Sartre (1955). At a particular moment, one of two women says to the other: "I'm your lark-mirror, my dear, and you can't escape me ... There isn't any pimple, not a trace of one. So what about it? Suppose the mirror started telling lies? Or suppose I covered my eyes – as he is doing – and refused to look at you, all that loveliness of yours would be wasted on the desert air" (p. 21).
4 "L'enfer est tout entier dans ce mot: Solitude" (The whole of hell is in this word: loneliness) – Victor Hugo, *La Fin de Satan* (1886).
5 Franz Kafka, "The Sudden Walk," translated by Willa Muir and Edwin Muir, in *Franz Kafka Stories*, http://franzkafkastories.com/shortStories.php?story_id=kafka_the_sudden_walk.
6 Would there be any linkage between this finding and the fact that since the sixties the number of people who live alone has doubled? Recent statistics show that one in two apartments in Paris is occupied by a lone renter (Lipovetsky and Serroy 2008, 60).
7 It is so easy to fill this privileged space with all the constraints in which we are enclosed, like the group of tourists just arrived (in Joseph

Conrad's novel): "An outward-bound mail-boat had come in that afternoon, and the big dining-room of the hotel was more than half full of people with a-hundred-pounds-round-the-world tickets in their pockets. There were married couples looking domesticated and bored with each other in the midst of their travels; there were small parties and large parties, and lone individuals dining solemnly or feasting boisterously, but all thinking, conversing, joking, or scowling as was their wont at home; and just as intelligently receptive of new impressions as their trunks upstairs. Henceforth they would be labeled as having passed through this and that place, and so would be their luggage. They would cherish this distinction of their persons, and preserve the gummed tickets on their portmanteaus as documentary evidence, as the only permanent trace of their improving enterprise" (Conrad 1899, *Lord Jim*, chap. 7).

8   It's interesting to see the work of Rineke Dijkstra, a Dutch photographer (b.1959). Her beach portraits, which generally feature one or more adolescents against a seascape in different countries, show how these young people try to present themselves as they are expected to.

9   We have all had the opportunity to observe that birds are more numerous in the city on Sunday morning, when life goes on at holiday rhythm.

10   "For the drama lies all in this – in the conscience that I have, that each one of us has. We believe this conscience to be a single thing, but it is many sided" (Pirandello, 1922).

11   "In order to approach that reality, a thought must be established in one's mind with sufficient authority to direct all the activities included for the achievement" of one's unique individuality, "the authority-thought will be, from then on, *the direct representative of one's conscience*" (González Pecotche 1996, 66).

12   In this sense we are all "worthy" sons of our common father, Adam, who answered to God about his disobedience, tit for tat: it was "the woman that you gave to be with me" (Genesis 3:11).

13   The Faust of Goethe realizes that nothing is acquired automatically, even what we have the chance to inherit: "What from your father you've inherited, / You must earn again, to own it straight." J.W. von Goethe, *Faust*, pt I, sc. 1, translated by A.S. Kline, 2003, in A.S. Kline, ed., *Poetry in Translation*, http://tkline.pgcc.net/PITBR/German/Fausthome.htm.

14 "In a place in which there is no struggle, there is no life." F.W. Schelling (1977, 147)

15 See in Bauman (2001), *The Individualized Society,* chap. 3, "Freedom and Security."

CHAPTER TWO

1 Maffesoli transforms the relatively narrow anthropological concept of tribe into one much broader and sociological, which identifies and describes as a postmodern phenomenon spanning national borders. In this regard, he observes that mass culture has disintegrated, leaving in its wake a diversity of "tribes." These tribes are fragmented groupings left over from the preceding era of rampant mass consumption, groupings recognized today by their unique tastes, lifestyles, and form of social organization.

CHAPTER THREE

1 "[I]t's quite clear that nowadays society is more a leisure one than a work one; the traffic of Friday or Saturday nights is much more important when people go to entertain themselves than in the morning of Monday when they go to work" (Dominico de Masi 2000).

2 We all have in mind what leaders have always known, that if they want approbation from their people, they have to provide *not only* "*panem*," bread, but also "*circenses*," circuses with their games (according to the famous verse of Juvenal, first century AD, *Satires* X, 81).

3 "Remorse," translated by A.S. Kline, 2008, A.S. Kline, ed., *Poetry in Translation,* http://www.poetryintranslation.com/PITBR/Spanish/Borges.htm.

4 The French mime, Marcel Marceau, in a famous small performance shows how a man changing his expression in accordance with the changing circumstances remains fixed with a large smile he can't remove (to see the performance: "Marcel Marceau Sketch," *YouTube,* 25 June 2008, http://www.youtube.com/watch?v=i99k7nCnVwM& feature=related.

5 *Persona* means in Latin, "mask," which in theatre fits some specific character.

6   Bertrand Russell, "In Praise of Idleness" (1932), http://www.zpub.com/
    notes/idle.html.

7   We remember that playing is essentially an interaction, both between
    people and within one's self. Solitaire and other games one plays alone
    are a kind of distortion, where the tacit aim of a game is, in general,
    human encounter and human sharing.

8   Arlecchino (Harlequin), used to always be the eternal servant with
    his peculiar dress, his familiar mask, and often accompanied by his
    beloved Columbina or Pantalone, the Venetian merchant, and the
    Dottore Gratiano always embarked on his amusing pedantic mixture
    of Italian and Latin.

9   Like Henry Higgins in G.B. Shaw's *Pygmalion*, who could guess where
    anybody lived according to their pronunciation.

10 "The people were at a feast, why? Do they know? No. They were told
    that they would be at a feast ... they were at a feast; they were content,
    they were happy. Until evening they will be joyful, by the Authorities'
    command, and tomorrow all that will be over." (de Maupassant [1886]
    1979, 1278–9).

CHAPTER FOUR

1   Of interest here is the fact that double-blind tests have demonstrated
    that local tap water is often identified by participants in experiments
    as tasting as good if not better than the commercially ballyhooed stuff
    in the bottle (Swartzberg 2007, 3).

CHAPTER FIVE

1   Bourdieu (179) explained that "legitimate" possessors of knowledge
    tend to hate the "vulgar," who deny their right to consume information
    directly.

2   "Let us remember that if the social circumstances did change, people
    still need belonging and identity. Most of us respond to the rooted ten-
    dency to conformism with a small difference: the predisposition to go
    with what goes doesn't serve any more only the defined and canonic
    traditions. The citizen-client (Touraine 1994) buy what appears as the
    most attractive in the market of the day?" (Cohen-Gewerc 2008, citing
    Touraine 1994).

3 Available at the *Perseus Digital Library*, ed. Gregory R. Crane, Tufts
   University, http://www.perseus.tufts.edu/hopper/text?doc=Perseus%3
   Atext%3A1999.01.0052%3Abook%3D1%3Asection%3D981b.

4 "There is a great difference between a poet seeking the particular
   for the universal, and seeing the universal in the particular. The one
   gives rise to Allegory, where the particular serves only as instance
   or example of the general; but the other is the true nature of Poetry,
   namely, the expression of the particular without any thought of, or
   reference to, the general. If a man grasps the particular vividly, he also
   grasps the general, without being aware of it at the time; or he may
   make the discovery long afterwards." *The Maxims and Reflections of
   Goethe*, §435, translated by Thomas Bailey Saunders, http://www.
   rodneyohebsion.com/goethe.htm.

5 We are told that, arriving at Princeton, Einstein requested a desk, a big
   pack of paper and a large waste paper basket to throw out all the silly
   things he would write.

6 "Time will be always man's great friend, but man must demonstrate
   his friendship by no duping I" (González Pecotche 1998, 42).

7 Consumption in postmodernity (unlike our definition in chap. 4) "is
   defined as a strenuous new form of capitalist social organization,
   where leisure and culture, formerly marginal activities for the majority of people, have been co-opted to the production process itself"
   (Wheale 1995, 10).

Bibliography

Applebaum, H. 1992. *The Concept of Work: Ancient, Medieval, and Modern*. Albany, NY: State University of New York Press.

Arai, S.M., and Pedlar, A.M. 1997. "Building Communities through Leisure: Citizen Participation in a Healthy Communities Initiative." *Journal of Leisure Research* 29: 167–82.

Aristotle. (1933) 1989. *Aristotle in 23 Volumes*, vols 17, 18. Translated by Hugh Tredennick. Cambridge, MA: Harvard University Press; London: William Heinemann Ltd. http://www.perseus.tufts.edu/hopper/text?doc=Perseus%3Atext%3A1999.01.0052%3Abook%3D1%3Asection%3D981b.

Auster, P. 1990. *City of Glass*, in *The New York Trilogy*. New York: Penguin Books.

Balzac, H. de. (1842–50) 1976. *La comédie humaine*, vol. 1. Paris: Éditions de la Nouvelle Revue Français.

Barber, B.R. 2007. *Consumed: How Markets Corrupt Children, Infantilize Adults, and Swallow Citizens Whole*. New York: W.W. Norton.

– 2008. "Think You Love Shopping? It's the Marketing Scam of the Century." Interview by S. Morris. *Independent* (London), 19 June, retrieved 11 January 2009. http://www.independent.co.uk/environment/green-living/think-you-love-shopping-its-the-marketing-scam-of-the-century-849922.html.

Bass, D., Wells, F., and Ridgeway, R. 1986. *Seven Summits*. New York: Warner Books.

Baudelaire, C. 1961. "Le flacon." In *Les fleurs du mal*. Paris: Le Livre de Poche.

Baudrillard, J. 1981. *For a Critique of the Political Economy of Signs.* Translated by C. Levin. New York: Telos Press.

Bauman, Z. 2001. *The Individualized Society.* Cambridge: Polity Press.

Beatrice, M. 2009. "Play as Rehearsal of Reality." In *Encyclopedia of Play in Today's Society*, edited by Rodney P. Carlisle, 537–8. Thousand Oaks, CA: Sage. http://www.sage-ereference.com/play/Article_n301.html.

Beck, U. 2000. *The Brave New World of Work.* Translated by P. Camiller. New York: Polity Press.

Belk, R. 2007. "Consumption, Mass Consumption, and Consumer Culture." In *The Blackwell Encyclopedia of the Social Sciences*, edited by G. Ritzer, 737–46. Cambridge, MA: Blackwell.

Betancourt, I. 2010. *Même le silence a une fin.* Paris: Éditions Gallimard.

Bergson, H. 1900. *Le rire.* Paris: Presses Universitaires de France. http://classiques.uqac.ca/classiques/bergson_henri/le_rire/Bergson_le_rire.doc.

– 1966. *L'Énergie spirituelle.* Paris: Presses Universitaires de France.

– 1983. *L'Évolution créatrice.* Paris: Presses Universitaires de France.

Berlin, Isaiah. 1969. *Four Essays on Liberty.* Oxford: Oxford University Press.

Binham, C. 2008. Yes, Guv'ner, UK Needs Butlers. *Calgary Herald*, Sunday, 13 April.

Bourdieu, P. 1977. *Outline of a Theory of Practice.* Translated by R. Nice. Cambridge: Cambridge University Press.

– 1979. *La distinction: Critique sociale du jugement.* Translated by R. Nice. Paris: Les Éditions de Minuit.

– 1987. *Les choses dites.* Paris: Les Éditions de Minuit.

Bramante, A.C. 2004. "Fostering Human Resources in the Leisure Field: 'Serious Leisure' and the Potential Role of Volunteers: A Proposal for Developing Countries." In *Volunteering as Leisure/Leisure as Volunteering: An International Assessment*, edited by R.A. Stebbins and M.M. Graham, 225–40. Wallingford: CAB International.

Branch, J. 2010. "Perfection in the Horseshoe Pit." *New York Times*, 20 July. http://www.nytimes.com/2010/07/21/sports/21horseshoe.html?pagewanted=all.

Buber, M. 1955. *Between Man and Man.* Translated by Ronald Gregor Smith. Boston: Beacon Press.

– 1958. *I and Thou*. Translated by Ronald Gregor Smith. New York: Charles Scribner's Sons.

Caillois, R. 1967. *Les jeux et les hommes: Le masque et le vertige*. Paris: Éditions Gallimard.

Cambridge Learner's Dictionary, 3rd ed. 2007. Cambridge: Cambridge University Press.

Camus, A. 1962. *L'Exil et le royaume*, in *Théâtre, récits, nouvelles*. Biblithèque de la Pléiade. Paris: Éditions de la Nouvelle Revue Français.

– 1965. *Caligula*, in *Caligula and Cross Purpose*. Translated by Stuart Gilbert. Harmondsworth: Penguin Books.

Cohen-Gewerc, E. 2008. "L'Ère du Loisir: Vers une nouvelle forme de vie communautaire." Paper presented at the 10th World Leisure Congress, Quebec City, 6–10 October.

– 2001. "Boredom, Threshold of Creative Leisure." *Gerontology* 30, nos 1–2: 87–95.

Cohen-Gewerc, E., and Spector, C. 2001 "From Education to Initiation: Leisure as a Second Chance." *World Leisure Journal* 43, no. 3: 48–53.

Cohen-Gewerc, E., and Stebbins, R. 2007. *The Pivotal Role of Leisure Education: A Manifesto for This Century*. State College, PA: Venture.

Cook, D.T. 2006. "Leisure and Consumption." In *A Handbook of Leisure Studies*, edited by C. Rojek, S.M. Shaw, and A.J. Veal, 304–16. New York: Palgrave Macmillan.

Cossu, A. 2009. "Sociology of Play as Entertainment." In *Encyclopedia of Play in Today's Society*, edited by Rodney P. Carlisle, 510–12. Thousand Oaks, CA: Sage. http://www.sage-ereference.com/play/Article_n292.html.

Cross, G. 1990. *A Social History of Leisure since 1600*. State College, PA: Venture.

Crouch, D. 2006 "Geographies of Leisure." In *A Handbook of Leisure Studies*, edited by C. Rojek, S.M. Shaw, and A.J. Veal, 125–39. Basingstoke: Palgrave Macmillan.

Csikszentmihalyi, M. 1990. *Flow: The Psychology of Optimal Experience*. New York: Harper & Row.

Cushman, G., Veal, A.J., and Zuzanek, J., eds. 2005. *Free Time and Leisure Participation: International Perspectives*. Wallingford: CAB International.

de Lamartine, Alphonse. 1920. *Oevres Choisies de Lamartine*. Paris: Bibliotheque Hachette.

Deleuze, G. 1993 *The Fold: Leibniz and the Baroque*. London: Athlone Press.

De Masi, D. 2000. *O Ocio Criativo*. Rio de Janeiro: Editora Sextante.

de Maupassant, Guy (1886) 1979. "Jour de fête." *Contes et nouvelles*. Bibliothèque de La Pléiade, vol. II. Edited by Louis Forestier. Paris: Gaullimard.

The Dictionary of Art Historians. 2010. Art History Webmasters Association, retrieved 17 March 2010. http://www.dictionaryofart historians.org/jarvesj.htm.

Diener, E., and Tov, W. 2007. "Subjective Well-Being and Peace." *Journal of Social Issues* 63: 421–40.

Dufrenne, M. 1967 *L'Expérience esthétique*. Paris: Presses Universitaires de France.

Duguid, H. 2008. "Shooting Stars: A Dazzling New Exhibition Explores How Hollywood Exploits the Power of Photography." *Independent* (London), 11 June. http://www.independent.co.uk/arts-entertainment/films/features/shooting-stars-a-dazzling-new-exhibition-explores-how-hollywood-exploits-the-power-of-photography-844053.html.

Dumazedier, J. 1993. "Epilogue." In *Temps libre et modernité: Mélanges en l'honneur de Joffre Dumazedier*. Québec, PQ: Presses de l'Université du Québec; Paris: Éditions L'Harmattan.

Economist. 2008. "Play On." 20 December.

Ehrenberg, A. 2000. *La fatigue d'être soi: Dépression et société*. Paris, Éditions Odile Jacob.

Falk, P., and Campbell, C. 1997. Introduction to *The Shopping Experience*, edited by P. Falk and C. Campbell, 1–14. London: Sage.

Foucault, M. 1984. *Le souci de soi*. Paris: Éditions Gallimard.

Fromm, E. 1941. *Escape from Freedom*. New York: Henry Holt Publishers.

Gelber, S.M. 1999. *Hobbies: Leisure and the Culture of Work in America*. New York: Columbia University Press.

Gergen, D. 2006. "The New Engines of Reform." *US News & World Report*, 2 December (online edition). http://www.usnews.com/usnews/biztech/articles/060220/20gergen.htm.

Giddens, A. 1986. *The Constitution of Society: Outline of the Theory of Structuration*. Berkeley, CA: University of California Press.

Goethe J.W. 1996. *Maximes et réflexions*, in *Ecrits sur l'art*. Paris: Éditions Flammarion.

González Pecotche, C.B. 1934. *Axiomas I*. Buenos Aires: Fundación Logosófica.

– 1962. *Deficiencias y Propensiones del ser humano*. Buenos Aires: Fundación Logosófica.

– 1996. *Logosophy, Science and Method*. São Paulo: Editora Logosófica.

– 1998. *An Introduction to Logosophical Cognition*. São Paulo: Editora Logosófica.

Gould, J., Moore, D., McGuire, F., and Stebbins, R.A. 2008. "Development of the Serious Leisure Inventory and Measure." *Journal of Leisure Research* 40, no. 1: 47–68.

Green, B.C., and Jones, I. 2005. "Serious Leisure, Social Identity and Sport Tourism." *Sport in Society* 8: 164–81.

Habermas, J. 1985. *Theory of Communicative Action: Reason and Rationalization of Society*, vol. 1. Translated by T. McCarthy. Boston: Beacon.

Hanoi Grapevine. 2009. "Trinh Cong Son's Music." June. Retrieved 23 March 2010. http://hanoigrapevine.com/2009/06/lang_ entrinh-cong-sons-musiclang_enlang_vitrinh-cong-sons-musiclang_vi.

Harris, M. 2008. "Look-at-Me Culture Wallowing in Competitive Compassion." *Calgary Herald*, 10 March.

Harrison, J. 2001. "Thinking about Tourists." *International Sociology* 16: 159–72.

Higham, J., and Hinch, T. 2009. "Mountain Climbing and Serious Leisure." In *Sport and Tourism: Globalisation, Mobility, and Identity*, edited by J. Higham and T. Hinch, 125–42. Oxford: Butterworth-Heinemann.

Hockett, J. 1999. "Burningman and the Ritual Aspects of Play." Michigan State University Web site. https://www.msu.edu/~hockettj/Play.htm.

Honneth, A. 1995. *The Struggle for Recognition: The Moral Grammar of Social Conflicts*. Translated by Joel Anderson. Cambridge, MA: MIT Press.

Hugo, V. (1886) 1999. *La fin de Satan*. Association de Bibliophiles Universels. http://abu.cnam.fr/cgi-bin/donner_html?satan1.

Huizinga, J. 1955. *Homo Ludens*. Boston, MA: Beacon.

Hunt, S. 2008. "But We're Men Aren't We!: Living History as a Site Of Masculine Identity Construction. *Men and Masculinities* 10, no. 4: 460–83.

Hutchinson, S.L., and Kleiber, D.A. 2005. "Gifts of the Ordinary: Casual Leisure's Contributions to Health and Well-Being." *World Leisure Journal* 47, no. 3: 2–16.

Ionesco, E. 1952. *La cantatrice chauve*, in *Théâtre*. Paris: Radiodiffusion Française.

Iso-Ahola, S.E. 2009. "Exercise and Freedom." *World Leisure Journal* 51, no. 3: 134–49.

Jankélévitch, V. 1963. *L'Aventure, l'ennui, le sérieux*. Paris: Éditions Aubier-Montaigne.

Jauss, H.R. 1978. *Pour une esthétique de la perception*. Paris: Éditions Gallimard.

Johnson, K. 2010. "Seeing Old Age as a Never-Ending Adventure." *New York Times*, 8 January. http://www.nytimes.com/2010/01/08/us/08aging.html.

Kandinsky, W. 1956. *Du spirituel dans l'art et dans la peinture en particulier*. Paris: Éditions de Beaune.

Kaplan, M. 1960. *Leisure in America: A Social Inquiry*. New York: Wiley.

– 1975. *Leisure: Theory and Policy*. New York: Wiley.

Kelly, J.R. 1987. *Freedom to Be: A New Sociology of Leisure*. New York: Macmillan.

– 1990. *Leisure*. 2nd ed. Englewood Cliffs, NJ: Prentice-Hall.

Keyes, C.L.M. 1998. "Social Well-Being." *Social Psychology Quarterly* 61: 121–40.

Kodas, M. 2008. *High Crime: The Fate of Everest in an Age of Greed*. New York: Hyperion.

Kranz, P. 2008. "Measuring Wealth by the Foot." *New York Times*, 16 March (online edition). http://www.nytimes.com/2008/03/16/business/16drop.html.

Lambdin, L. 1997. *Elderlearning*. Phoenix, AZ: Oryx Press.

Lefebvre, H. 1991. *Critique of Everyday Life*, vol. 1: *Introduction*. Translated by J. Moore. London: Verso.

Light, P.C. 2008. *The Search for Social Entrepreneurship*. Washington,
DC: Brookings Institution Press.

Lipovetsky, G., and Serroy, J. 2008. *La culture-monde: Réponse à une
société désorientée*. Paris: Éditions Odile Jacob.

Lombry, T. 2010. "The History of Amateur Radio." *Luxorion* Web site,
retrieved 17 March 2010. http://www.astrosurf.com/luxorion/qsl-
ham-history6.htm.

Madehow.com 2010. "Grote Reber Biography (1911–)." http://www.
madehow.com/inventorbios/96/Grote-Reber.html#ixzz0ju7n1LFM.

Maffesoli, M. 1996. *The Time of the Tribes: The Decline of Individualism*. Translated by D. Smith. London: Sage.

Mannell, R.C. 1999. "Leisure Experience and Satisfaction." In *Leisure Studies: Prospects for the Twenty-First Century*, edited by E.L.
Jackson and T.L. Burton, 235–52. State College, PA: Venture.

Martel, F. 2006. *De la culture en Amérique*. Paris: Éditions Gallimard.

Martin, B., and Mason, S. 1987. "Current Trends in Leisure." *Leisure
Studies* 6: 93–7.

McCarthy, M. 2010. "Safe-Bet Winter Olympics Stars Could See
Endorsements Spike." *USA Today*, 1 March (online edition). http://
www.usatoday.com/sports/olympics/2010-03-01-olympians-
endorsements_N.htm.

McClay, W.M. 2009. "David Riesman and *The Lonely Crowd*." *Society* 46, no. 1: 21–8 (online edition). http://www.springerlink.com/
content/0147-2011/48/3/?MUD=MP.

McDonald, M., Wearing, S., and Ponting, J. 2007. "Narcissism and
Neo-Liberalism: Work, Leisure, and Alienation in an Era of Consumption." *Society and Leisure* 30: 489–510.

McKinley, J. 2012. "Space Tourism Is Here! Wealthy Adventurers
Wanted." *New York Times*, 8 September (online edition). http://
www.nytimes.com/2012/09/09/travel/space-tourism-is-here-wealthy-
adventurers-wanted.html.

Misrahi, R. 1981. *Construction d'un château*. Paris: Éditions du Seuil.

Nietzsche, F. 1911. *The Dawn of Day*. Translated by John McFarland
Kennedy. New York: Macmillan. http://www.gutenberg.org/
files/39955/39955-h/39955-h.html.

– 1896. *Thus Spake Zarathustra*. Translated by Thomas Common.
Gutenburg EBook, 2008. http://www.gutenberg.org/files/1998/
1998-h/1998-h.htm.

Packer, J. 2006. "Learning for Fun: The Unique Contribution of Educational Leisure Experiences. *Curator: The Museum Journal* 49, no. 3: 329–44.

Parker, S. 1983. *Leisure and Work*. London: George Allen & Unwin.

Pedlar, A. 1996. "Community Development: What Does It Mean for Recreation and Leisure." *Journal of Applied Recreation Research* 21: 5–23.

Pirandello, L. 1922. *Naked Masks: Five Plays*. Edited by Eric Bentley. New York: E.P. Dutton.

Ploch, L. 1976. "Community Development in Action: A Case Study." *Journal of Community Development and Society* 7: 5–16.

Prus, R., and Dawson, L. 1991. "Shop 'til You Drop: Shopping as Recreational and Laborious Activity." *Canadian Journal of Sociology* 16: 145–64.

Putnam, R.D. 2000. *Bowling Alone: The Collapse and Revival of American Community*. New York: Simon & Schuster.

Riesman, D. 1961. *The Lonely Crowd: A Study of the Changing American Character*. Rev. ed. New Haven, CT: Yale University Press.

Roberson, D.N., Jr. 2005. "Leisure and Learning: An Investigation of Older Adults and Self-Directed Learning." *Leisure* 29: 203–38.

Roberts, K. 1997. "Same Activities, Different Meanings: British Youth Cultures in the 1990s." *Leisure Studies* 16: 1–16.

Robinson, J.P., and Godbey, G. 1997. *Time for Life: The Surprising Ways Americans Use Their Time*. University Park, PA: Pennsylvania State University Press.

Robinson, J. P., and Martin, S. 2008. "What Do Happy People Do?" *Social Indicators Research* 89: 565–71.

Rogers, E. M. 2003. *Diffusion of Innovations*. 5th ed. New York: Free Press.

Rojek, C. 2000. *Leisure and Culture*. London: Palgrave.

– 2002. "Civil Labour, Leisure and Post Work Society." *Society and Leisure* 25: 21–36.

Rousseau, J.-J. 1992. *The Reveries of the Solitary Walker*. Translated by Ch.E. Butterworth. Indianapolis: Hackett. http://books.google.com/books?id=dYlkKJoCHnEC&printsec=frontcover&hl=iw&source=gbs_ge_summary_r&cad=0#v=onepage&q&f=true.

Salvato, F. 2007. "The Acceptance of Thuggery for Fun, Power and Profit." *American Chronicle*, 1 September, retrieved 17 March 2010. http://www.americanchronicle.com/articles/view/36447.

Sartre, J.-P. 1943. *l'Être et le néant*. Paris: Éditions Gallimard.

– 1955. *No Exit and Three Other Plays*. Translated by Stuart Gilbert and Lionel Abel. New York: Vintage books.

– 1984. *Search for the Absolute*, in *Four Articles*. Tel Aviv: Sifriat Hapoalim Press.

Schelling, F.W. 1977. *Recherches sur la liberté humaine*. Paris: Éditions Payot.

Schiller, F. (1794) 1909–14. *On the Aesthetic Education of Man in a Series of Letters*. Harvard Classics. Edited by Charles W. Eliot. New York: P.F. Collier & Son. Bartleby.com. http://www.bartleby.com/32/503.html.

Schlesinger, V. 2008. "The Amateur Scientists Who Might Cure Cancer – From Their Basements." *Discover Magazine* (December), online 19 November 2008. http://discovermagazine.com/2008/dec/ 19-the-amateur-scientists-who-might-cure-cancer-from-their-basements.

Schopenhauer, A. (1893) 2007. " Personality, or What a Man Is." In *Parerga and Paralipomena: A Collection of Philosophical Essays*. New York: Cosimo.

– 1909. *The World as Will and Idea*, vol. 1. Translated by R.B. Haldane and J. Kemp. 7th ed. London: Kegan Paul, Trench, Trübner & Co. Gutenberg EBook, 2011. http://www.gutenberg.org/files/38427/38427-h/38427-h.html.

Seeman, M. 1972. "Alienation and Engagement." In *The Human Meaning of Social Change*, edited by A. Campbell and P.E. Converse, 467–527. New York: Russell Sage Foundation.

Selman, G., Cooke, M., Selman, M., and Dampier, P. 1998. *The Foundations of Adult Education in Canada*. 2nd ed. Toronto, ON: Thompson.

Silverberg, S. 2008. "Employee Perceptions of Organizational Commitment: An Exploratory Study." PhD thesis, Department of Sociology, University of Calgary.

Simmel, G. 1989. *Philosophie de la modernité: La femme, la ville, l'individualisme*. Paris: Éditions Payot.

Smith, D.H., Stebbins, R.A., and Dover, M. 2006. *A Dictionary Of Nonprofit Terms and Concepts*. Bloomington, IN: Indiana University Press.

Snyder, C.R., and Lopez, J. 2007. *Positive Psychology: The Scientific And Practical Explorations of Human Strengths*. Thousand Oaks, CA: Sage.

Somers, M.R. 1993. "Citizenship and the Place of the Public Sphere: Law, Community and Political Culture in the Transition to Democracy." *American Sociological Review* 58: 587–621.

Stebbins, R.A. 1972. "Modesty, Pride, and Conceit: Variations in the Expression of Self-Esteem." *Pacific Sociological Review* 15: 461–81.

– 1981. "The Social Psychology of Selfishness." *Canadian Review of Sociology and Anthropology* 18: 82–92.

– 1990. *The Laugh-Makers: Stand-Up Comedy as Art, Business, and Life-Style*. Montreal: McGill-Queen's University Press.

– 1992. *Amateurs, Professionals, and Serious Leisure*. Montreal and Kingston: McGill-Queen's University Press.

– 1995. "Leisure and Selfishness: An Exploration." In *Reflections on the Philosophy of Leisure*, vol. II: *Leisure and Ethics*, edited by G.S. Fain, 292–303. Reston, VA: American Alliance for Health, Physical Education, Recreation, and Dance.

– 1996a. *The Barbershop Singer: Inside the Social World of A Musical Hobby*. Toronto: University of Toronto Press.

– 1996b. *Tolerable Differences: Living with Deviance*. 2nd ed. Toronto: McGraw-Hill Ryerson.

– 1996c. "Volunteering: A Serious Leisure Perspective." *Nonprofit and Voluntary Sector Quarterly* 25: 211–24.

– 1998. *The Urban Francophone Volunteer: Searching for Personal Meaning and Community Growth in a Linguistic Minority*, vol. 3, no. 2. New Scholars–New Visions in Canadian Studies (quarterly monographs series). Seattle, WA: University of Washington, Canadian Studies Center.

– 2001. *New Directions in the Theory and Research of Serious Leisure*. Mellen Studies in Sociology, vol. 28. Lewiston, NY: Edwin Mellen.

– 2002. *The Organizational Basis of Leisure Participation: A Motivational Exploration*. State College, PA: Venture.

– 2003. "Boredom in Free Time." *Leisure Studies Association Newsletter* 64 (March), 29–31. Also available at Serious Leisure Perspective, Leisure Reflections 2. http://www.seriousleisure.net/uploads/8/3/3/8/8338986/reflections2.pdf.

– 2004a. *Between Work and Leisure: The Common Ground of Two Separate Worlds*. New Brunswick, NJ: Transaction.

- 2004b. "Pleasurable Aerobic Activity: A Type of Casual Leisure with Salubrious Implications." *World Leisure Journal* 46, no. 4: 55–8.
- 2005a. "Choice and Experiential Definitions of Leisure." *Leisure Sciences* 27: 349–52.
- 2005b. *Challenging Mountain Nature: Risk, Motive, and Lifestyle in Three Hobbyist Sports.* Calgary: Detselig.
- 2006a "Contemplation as Leisure and Non-leisure." *Leisure Studies Association Newsletter* 73 (March): 16–18. Also available at Serious Leisure Perspective, Leisure Reflections 11. http://www.serious leisure.net/uploads/8/3/3/8/8338986/reflections11.pdf.
- 2006b. "Discretionary Time Commitment: Effects on Leisure Choice and Lifestyle." *Leisure Studies Association Newsletter* 74 (July): 18–20. Also available at Serious Leisure Perspective, Leisure Reflections 12. http://www.seriousleisure.net/uploads/8/3/3/8/8338986/reflections12.pdf.
- 2007. *Serious Leisure: A Perspective for Our Time.* New Brunswick, NJ: Transaction.
- 2009. *Personal Decisions in the Public Square: Beyond Problem Solving into a Positive Sociology.* New Brunswick, NJ: Transaction.
- 2010a. "Social Entrepreneurship as Work and Leisure." *Leisure Studies Association Newsletter* 85 (March): 30–3. Also available at Serious Leisure Perspective, Leisure Reflections 23. http://www.seriousleisure.net/uploads/8/3/3/8/8338986/reflections23.pdf.
- 2010b. "Addiction to Leisure Activities: Is It Possible?" *Leisure Studies Association Newsletter* 86 (July): 19–22. Also available at Serious Leisure Perspective, Leisure Reflections 24. http://www.seriousleisure.net/uploads/8/3/3/8/8338986/reflections_24.pdf.
- 2011. "Personal Memoirs, Project-Based Leisure and Therapeutic Recreation for Seniors." *Leisure Studies Association Newsletter* 88 (March): 29–31. Also available at Serious Leisure Perspective, Leisure Reflections 26. http://www.seriousleisure.net/uploads/8/3/3/8/8338986/reflections26.pdf.
- 2012. *The Idea of Leisure: First Principles.* New Brunswick, NJ: Transaction.
Suetonius, T. n.d. *The Lives of the Twelve Caesars.* Translated by A. Thomson, revised by T. Forester. Gutenberg Ebook, 2006. http://www.gutenberg.org/files/6400/6400-h/6400-h.htm.

Swartzberg, J. 2007. Bottled Water Bites the Dust. *Wellness Letter* (University of California, Berkeley) 23, no. 12: 3.

Taylor, C. 1989. *Sources of the Self: The Making of the Modern Identity.* Cambridge, MA: Harvard University Press.

– *The Malaise of Modernity.* Toronto: House of Anansi Press.

Teilhard de Chardin, P. 1955. *Le phénomène humain.* Paris: Éditions du Seuil.

Touraine, A. 1994. *Qu'est-ce que la démocratie.* Paris: Éditions Fayard.

– 2005. *Un nouveau paradigme pour comprendre le monde d'aujourd'hui.* Paris: Éditions Fayard.

Tsaur, S.-H., and Liang, Y.-W. 2008. "Serious Leisure and Recreation Specialization." *Leisure Sciences* 30, no. 4: 325–41.

Unruh, D.R. 1980. "The Nature of Social Worlds." *Pacific Sociological Review* 23: 271–96.

Veblen, T. 1899. *The Theory of the Leisure Class: An Economic Study of Institutions.* New York: Macmillan.

Wearing, S., and McDonald, M. 2003. "Commodification." In *Encyclopedia of Leisure and Outdoor Recreation,* edited by J.M. Jenkins and J.J. Pigram, 60–1. London: Routledge.

Wheale, N., ed. 1995. *The Postmodern Arts: An Introductory Reader.* London: Routledge.

Wilensky, R. 1978. "A Conceptual Analysis of the Verbs *Need* and *Want.*" *Cognitive Science* 2: 391–6.

Williams, R.M., Jr. 2000. "American Society." In *Encyclopedia of Sociology.* 2nd ed., edited by E.F. Borgatta and R.J.V. Montgomery, vol. 1, 140–8. New York: Macmillan.

Wragg, M. 2009. "Sociological Benefits of Play." In *Encyclopedia of Play in Today's Society,* edited by Rodney P. Carlisle, 663–5. Thousand Oaks, CA: Sage. http://www.sage-ereference.com/play/Article_n378.html.

Yardley, J. 2010. "For India's Newly Rich Farmers, Limos Won't Do." *New York Times,* 18 March (online edition). http://www.nytimes.com/2010/03/19/world/asia/19india.html?_r=1.

Index

activity, 34–7; core, 36–7
agency-structure debate, 152–4
Applebaum, Herbert, 31
art and leisure, 103; authentic
    appeal of, 106; changing con-
    tours of life's vitality, 110;
    dialogue, as creation of, 111;
    demanding effort and cour-
    age, 108; and marketing, 103;
    motivated to create, 107; as an
    oasis, 117; offering a renewed
    vision, 112–13; useless, 108;
    vulgarization of, 104
Aristotle, 107
Auster, Paul, 64

Barber, Bernard R., 97
Bass, Dick, 98
Baudelaire, Charles, 21
Baudrillard, Jean, 96
Bauman, Zygmunt, 159n15
Beatrice, Maria, 70
Beck, Ulrich, ix, 131
Beethoven, Ludwig van, 110
Belk, Russell, 81
Bergson, Henri, 18, 22, 79, 113

Betancourt, Ingrid, 154
boredom, 32–3, 58
Bourdieu, Pierre, 87, 104, 148,
    153–4, 160n1
Bramante, Antonio C., 131
Buber, Martin, 7, 18, 26, 27, 106

Caillois, Roger, 72
Campbell, Colin, 91
Camus, Albert, 15, 76
casual leisure, 38, 45; community
    participation as, 128–9, 131–2;
    definition of, 37; identity and,
    56, 58; individuality through,
    50, 57–8, 100; shopping as, 92;
    values and, 138
Cezanne, Paul, 108
Cohen-Gewerc, Elie, 33, 117,
    160n2; and Spector, Corinne,
    106; and Stebbins, Robert,
    116, 156
community, 119–34; aliena-
    tion from, 119–27; conceit
    in, 125–7; exploitation and,
    121–3; immorality (deviance)
    and, 124–5; misrepresentation

and, 123–4; participation in, 120, 127–34; social capital and, 130–5; social well-being and, 138–9; values and, 136–8
consumption, 81–100; adopting innovations as, 87–8, 99; competitive compassion as, 89–91, 99–100; conspicuous, 84–7; definition of, 81; individuated identity through, 83–95; leisure and, 81–100; needs and, 95–9; selfishness in, 98–9; shopping as, 91–3; tourism as, 93–5; wants and, 95–8
Conrad, Joseph, 157–8n7
Cook, Daniel T., 81
Cooke, Michael, 53
Cossu, Andrea, 72, 75
Cross, Gary, 31
Crouch, David, 34
Cushman, Grant, 32

D'Alembert, Jean 103
Dampier, Paul, 53
Dawson, Lorne, 91, 92
de Lamartine, Alphonse, 77
Deleuze, Gilles, 117
De Masi, Dominico, 159n1
de Maupassant, Guy, 160n10
Diderot, Denis, 103
Diener, Edward, 138–9
Dijkstra, Rineke, 158n8
discretionary time commitment, 32
domains, 31
Dover, Michael, 120, 131
Duchamp, Marcel, 74
Dufrenne, Mikel, 107

Duguid, Herbert, 123

Ehrenberg, Alain, 14

Falk, Pasi, 91
Foucault, Michel, 77
freedom, 5; alone with, 20; and being free, 11; as a challenge, 6, 12; oblige, 21; overused, misused, manipulated, 12; and permissiveness, 15; and responsibility, 7, 25, 102; and uniqueness, 16
Fromm, Erich, 102

Garcia Lorca, Federico, 109
Gelber, Seven M., 31
Gergen, David, 133
Giacommetti, Alberto, 109, 110
Giddens, Anthony, 153
Godbey, Geoffrey, 32
Goethe, Johann Wolfgang von, 158n13, 161n4
González Pecotche, Carlos B., 7, 9, 22–3, 26–7, 75, 150–2, 158n11, 161n6
Gould, James, 133
Green, Christine, B., 56

Habermas, Jürgen, 153
Harris, Misty, 89
Harrison, Julie, 36
Heraclitus, 25
Highham, James, 56
Hinch, Tom, 56
Hockett, Jeremy, 75
Honneth, Axel, 6, 103
Hugo, Victor, 157n4

Huizinga, Johan, 59, 65, 75
Hunt, Stephen J., 56
Hutchinson, Susan L., 56

identity, 8; ready-to-wear, 8, 101;
    stable, 9
individuality (individuation), 8;
    achieved and ascribed, 145–7;
    through agency, 51–2, 59;
    authenticity in, 54–5; through
    citizenship and, 134–9; con-
    ceit and, 61–2, 65; as desire to
    sense our being, 115; identity
    through, 55–7, 65; fulfillment
    in, 53–4; globalization and,
    139–43; importance of, 147–8;
    through leisure, 49–57; neces-
    sities and, 52–3; preferences
    for, 50–1; reasons for, 148–50;
    selfishness and, 59–61, 65,
    98–9; two faces of, 100; under-
    mining, 57–62; through volun-
    teering, 121, 130–2, 136. See
    also agency-structure debate;
    community; consumption
Ionesco, Eugene, 17
Iso-Ahola, Seppo E., 15

Jankélévitch, Vadimir, 20–1
Johnson, Kirk, 95
Jones, Ian, 56

Kafka, Franz, 14, 157n5
Kandinsky, Wassily, 105, 107
Kaplan, Max, 29, 33
Keis, Kelly, 126
Kelly, John R., 30, 52, 55–6, 105
Keyes, Corey L.M., 138

Kleiber, Douglas A., 56
Kodas, Michael, 94
Kranz, Patricia, 85–6
Kubrick, Stanley, 69

Lambdin, Lois, 53
Lefebvre, Henri, 97
leisure, 8–10; definition of, 31;
    history of, 30–1; as institution,
    29–31. See also casual leisure;
    leisure space; project-based lei-
    sure; serious leisure
leisure space, 29–34; geographic
    space, 33–4; institutional
    space, 29–31; temporal space,
    32–3
Liang, Ying-Wen, 133
Light, Paul C., 130
Linton, Ralph, 145
Lipovetsky, Gilles, and Serroy,
    Jean, 16, 26, 115, 157n6
Lombry, Thierry, 128
Lopez, Shane J., 54
Luther, Martin, 104

Maffesoli, Michel, 50, 83, 132–3,
    159n1
Mannell, Roger C., 32
Marceau, Marcel, 159n4
Martel, Frédéric, 103
Martin, Bill, 93
Martin, Steven, 91
Mason, Sandra, 93
McCarthy, Mary, 142
McClay, Wilfred M., 148
McDonald, Matthew, 81, 95
McGuire, Francis, 133
McKinley, Jesse, 94

Michelangelo, Buonarroti, 103, 111

Moore, DeWayne, 133

Nietzsche, Friedrich, 16, 78

obligation, 31–2, 91, 93, 96–8

occupational devotion, 47–9; criteria of, 48–9; definition of, 47; individuality and, 49–57

Packer, Jan, 106

Parker, Stan, 52

Pedlar, Alison, 59

Picasso, Pablo, 110

Pirandello, Luigi, 158n10

play, 64; as creation, 78; as distraction, 68; as domesticated within boundaries, 75; as exploration, 70; life's experience, opening and enlarging of, 73; as necessity, 68; as re-creation, 77; serious leisure, an introduction to, 76

Ploch, Lawrence, 59

Ponting, Jess, 81

project-based leisure, 38, 45–7; communal, 135–6; community participation as, 129–30, 132, 135–6; as conspicuous consumption, 86; definition of, 37; identity and, 57; individuality through, 50–1, 100; motivation in, 149–50; values and, 138

Prus, Robert, 91, 92

Putnam, Robert D., 133

Ridgeway, Rick, 98

Riesman, David, 145, 147–8

Roberson Jr., Donald N., 53

Roberts, Ken, 58

Robinson, John P., 32, 91

Rogers, Everett M., 87

Rojek, Chris, 29, 130–1

Rousseau, Jean-Jacques, 24

Russell, Bertrand, 68, 160n6

Salvato, Frank, 126–7

Saramago, José, 110

Sartre, Jean-Paul, 6, 12, 109, 157n3

Schelling, Friedrich W., 159n14

Schiller, Friedrich, 8, 65, 79, 116

Schlesinger, Victor, 141

Schopenhauer, Arthur, 106, 116

Seeman, Melvin, 119–20

selfishness, 59–61, 98–9; alienation through, 120–1

Selman, Gordon, 53

Selman, Mark, 53

serious leisure, 38–45; career in, 53–4; definition of, 37; flow in, 43–5; globalization and, 140–3; individuality through 50–1, 100; motivation in, 41–3, 143–4, 149–50; shopping as, 92–3; six qualities of, 40–1; social capital as, 130–1, 133; values and, 137–8

serious leisure perspective, 37–49; definition of, 37

serious pursuits, 38, 39. See also serious leisure

Shakespeare, William, 78

Shaw, George Bernard, 160n9
Silverberg, Shane, 55
Simmel, Georg, 6
Smith, David H., 120, 131
Snyder, C.R., 54
Somers, Margaret R., 134
Stebbins, Robert A., 31–2, 37–49,
    53–4, 59–62, 76, 92, 98, 120–
    1, 125–6, 130–2, 133, 141–2,
    144, 147
Suetonius, 15, 67
Swartzberg, John, 160n1
Taylor, Charles, 7, 54
Teilhard de Chardin, Pierre, 26
Touraine, Alain, 16, 19, 21,
    115–16, 160n2
Tov, William, 138–9
Tsaur, Sheng-Hshiung, 133

Veal, Anthony J., 32
Veblen, Thorstein, 84–7, 89–91,
    123
Vermeer, Johannes, 112–14
Verneuil, Henri, 113

Wearing, Stephen, 81, 95
Wells, Frank, 98
Wheale, Nigel, 161n7
Wilensky, Robert, 95
Williams Jr., Robin M., 50, 137
work, 31; as occupational
    devotion, 47–9
Wragg, Mike, 65, 75

Yardley, Jim, 130

Zuzanek, Jiri, 32